Seeking Paradise
A Unitarian Mission For Our Times

Stephen Lingwood

The Lindsey Press
London

Published by the Lindsey Press
on behalf of the General Assembly of Unitarian
and Free Christian Churches
Essex Hall, 1–6 Essex Street, London WC2R 3HY, UK

© General Assembly of Unitarian and Free Christian Churches 2020

ISBN 978-0-85319-094-3

Designed and typeset by Garth Stewart

Front-cover image: a section of a mural ('Forest Scene') by Ivon Hitchens (1893–1979) in the Unitarian church in Golders Green. Reproduced by permission of John Hitchens; photograph © Peter D. Kyte

Contents

Foreword

For me, as the still-new Chief Officer of the General Assembly of Unitarian and Free Christian Churches, with the specific remit of guiding the transformation and growth of Unitarianism, the publication of this book is perfectly timed. What might the future of the Unitarian movement look like? That depends, it seems to me, on how we envision – and enact – its mission.

I believe that many of the ideas presented in this book will guide us in finding our place in contemporary society. Having heard about Stephen Lingwood's pioneering work as a minister in inner-city Cardiff soon after I took on my role (and having been told by some people, in slightly warning tones, "he's at the very *Christian* end of things"), I visited him in Cardiff in summer 2019. I was immediately excited by the power of the deep, slow work he is doing there – work that is inspired by the ideas set out in this book.

I suspect that many people in today's secular culture – including many Unitarians – may find some of the language in these pages challenging. Words and concepts such as "theology", "missiology", "evangelism", even "paradise", might seem at odds with prevailing culture, or come with baggage because of the type of religious association that is conventionally associated with them. (Indeed, when I myself first attended a Unitarian service, even simple words like "church" and "hymn" made me feel slightly queasy, and I only got through the door because I knew that the minister was an atheist.)

Stephen Lingwood shares very clearly how his own personal sense of mission is inseparable from his relationship with God and Jesus. This is very far from my own experience of Unitarianism – I feel I know relatively little about Jesus or the Bible – and yet the work that Stephen is doing in Cardiff, and the ideas that drive it, resonate very powerfully with me.

This, I feel, is a great value of Unitarianism: that we can find what we share beneath the traditions and between the different beliefs or lack of belief; and it will be essential for us if we are to increase our positive benefit to society. Although it took me a while, I am pleased that I am now comfortable doing the necessary translation work to find what makes sense for me when I hear someone talk about their relationship with God, and I can usually find a felt sense of the common ground.

My experience is that spirituality is universally human, even though we may each use very different language and ideas to explain and express it. Stephen Lingwood's ministry inspires me, and I believe it is an important model for what the future of Unitarianism might look like. That is not to say, of course, that we must all adopt his theological viewpoint; but I do believe that good work happens when it is driven by the courage of conviction, whether inspired by a relationship with Jesus or by something else.

Although its vision is presented through the lens of Unitarianism, I think this book has value for anyone working with communities, whether faith-based or otherwise. The mission-driven community building described here, which balances head, heart, and soul, which transcends individualism, and which operates outside the rigid and unnatural old power structures, is something that our society desperately needs more of. The couple of centuries since the emergence of Unitarianism in the age of Enlightenment and industrialisation have been uniquely damaging to our paradise of planet Earth, and the work of community building is essential to us if we are to find our way through.

One of the things that excites me most about this book is that it shows that evangelism need not be something to be scared of. Whether it is the example of my own missionary grandparents, or my work on marketing strategies in my earlier career, it seems obvious to me that if you value something it makes sense to tell people about it. I have been perplexed by the view that "Unitarians don't do evangelism", but it helps to explain why our numbers have dwindled so much. Telling people what we can offer is, of course, not the same as telling people what to believe. And if we really believe that what we do is valuable, we will do the work and invite the dialogue that means we can offer it in a way that resonates with the lives of those around us.

I believe that Unitarianism will flourish only if the work of each of us is driven by a clear personal mission, and with a sense of loving generosity rather than institutional self-preservation. In *Seeking Paradise*, Stephen Lingwood paints a picture which I hope readers will find inspirational.

Elizabeth Slade
January 2020

Acknowledgements

I would like to record my thanks to the congregation of Bank Street Unitarian Chapel in Bolton for granting me sabbatical leave in 2016. The sabbatical allowed me to do the lion's share of the work on this book. I am deeply grateful for the opportunity that I was given to think, read, and write. Thank you.

I also thank Jane Blackall for helping to draft the questions for reflection and discussion at the end of each chapter, and Kay Millard and Catherine Robinson for their editorial work.

For the front cover, John Hitchens kindly granted permission for the reproduction of a portion of the 'Forest Scene' mural by Ivon Hitchens, installed in the Golders Green Unitarian Church. Peter D. Kyte provided the photograph. My thanks are due to them both.

Stephen Lingwood

About the author

Stephen Lingwood is a minister serving the congregation of Cardiff Unitarians / Undodiaid Caerdydd and doing pioneering grass-roots mission work in inner-city Cardiff. Previously he worked for nine years as minister of Bank Street Unitarian Chapel in Bolton. He edited the book *The Unitarian Life: Voices from the Past and Present* (Lindsey Press, 2008) and has published several articles in journals including *Faith and Freedom* and *The Journal of Bisexuality*. He works in Riverside, a diverse, inner-city area of Cardiff, creating dialogue with artists and political radicals, working on climate activism, and collaborating with other faith-based activists. He is exploring what it means to seek paradise in one urban neighbourhood in the age of the climate crisis.

Introduction: What is the mission of Unitarianism?

Inch by inch, row by row,
gonna make this garden grow.
All it takes is a rake and a hoe,
and a piece of fertile ground.

"The Garden Song" by Dave Mallet
(Number 19 in *Unisongs*)

"In order to survive, there is an absolute need for numerical growth"

It was 2006, and for the first time ever I was attending the Annual Meetings of Unitarians in Britain, held that year on the campus of the University of Chester. I was the voting delegate for my congregation, and so I dutifully and enthusiastically attended all the business meetings. At one of those business meetings in a large lecture hall I sat and witnessed those assembled debating the following motion:

> That this General Assembly of Unitarian and Free Christian
> Churches acknowledges that, in order to survive, there is an
> absolute need for numerical growth. It urges every Unitarian
> organisation and member thereof to give high priority to numerical
> growth and to publicise this intention. It requests the General
> Assembly Executive Committee to set up an organisation and
> process that will bring together those who seek to promote
> numerical growth, where ideas, proven or not, can be exchanged,
> discussed and acted upon.[1]

I held up my voting card and voted for this motion; so did many others, and it passed overwhelmingly. The argument for it seemed strong. It seemed pretty clear that "in order to survive" growth was needed.

The picture was clear enough for anyone with eyes to see. The Unitarian community, along with many other denominations in Great Britain, had suffered from a general decline in religious adherence in the twentieth century.[2] Reliable statistics are hard to come by, but one source estimates a 79 per cent decline in Unitarian membership in the twentieth century.[3] This is probably not very different from many other religious groups, but Unitarians were starting with very small numbers. There were about 15,000 Unitarians in England, Wales, and Scotland in the 1980s, but by 2006 there were fewer than 4,000. Since then numbers have continued to shrink, and currently there are probably fewer than 3,000.[4]

We can always argue about the reliability and interpretation of statistics, but the overall picture of decline is one that cannot be denied. As one American observer has put it, "At best, it appears that British Unitarianism has another three generations before it dies."[5] Some may think that even this is over-optimistic. The 2006 resolution sought to address this decline by making it a national priority to seek to reverse it.

And yet, at the time, and more so in the years since, I have found myself coming back to the question: *why?* Why do we want to grow? The answer comes back: in order to survive. But then why is the survival of the Unitarian community a good thing? Why does it matter, other than for internal selfish reasons such as the fact that it currently employs people like me (as I am now a Unitarian minister)? But why should the world care? What is the Unitarian community *for?* What is its overall purpose or mission?

That is the question of this book. In theological terms it is the question of *missiology*, the question of the work of a religious community, its justification for existing, and its justification for promoting itself and seeking new members. What is the Unitarian theology of mission and evangelism and numerical growth?

And yet to begin to speak in these terms is to encounter immediate resistance. Such terms have associations with conservative, even fundamentalist, forms of Christianity. (These terms, and related expressions, can be confusing, so let me make a distinction here in how I will use them.

When I say *"Evangelical"* with a capital "E", I am referring to a particular type of Christianity that emphasises the authority of the Bible and the importance of personal conversion, and tends to be socially conservative. When I use the term *"evangelism"* with a lower case "e", I am referring to a particular practice that has something to do with growing churches. This sort of evangelism does not belong exclusively to Evangelicalism. So I am claiming that you can do evangelism without being an Evangelical.) Unitarianism is a very different kind of religious tradition from fundamentalist or Evangelical Christianity. And this is not simply a matter of language: it is one of deep and foundational theological commitments. The Unitarian tradition is universalist and pluralist, rather than exclusivist. In simple terms this means that we don't believe that going to heaven depends on your coming to our church, or committing to our faith. Nor do we believe that our religious path is the only true one.

If Unitarians do not believe that they are the sole bearers of truth and salvation, the question remains: why does Unitarianism matter? What reasons do we Unitarians have to be concerned with church growth, with our own existence, if truth and salvation do not depend upon it?

The 2006 motion was passed. And since then the Unitarian denomination has seemed to be constantly worrying about church growth and promotion (even though such preoccupations have rarely produced any positive results), while still maintaining a theology that seems, at first glance at least, to be saying the opposite.

This is the apparent contradiction that I want to try to solve. I want to ask whether mission, evangelism, and church growth belong inevitably to orthodox or conservative forms of religion, or whether such terms can be meaningful in a thoroughly liberal theological context.

To answer that question comprehensively requires the creation of a Unitarian missiology, a complete theology of mission. And that is what this book attempts to do. It is an attempt to draw upon the deep roots of a living tradition to see what resources exist in order to begin to answer the question of Unitarian purpose.

I believe it is only by answering the question of our purpose that we can begin to answer the question of our growth. It is only by answering the "why" question that we can begin to approach the "how" question. Indeed, our understanding of "why" will inevitably shape our understanding of "how". In other words, we can't talk about church growth without doing theology.

So, to briefly outline the journey that I am inviting the reader to take with me: I will begin this task of constructing a Unitarian sense of mission by surveying the concept and practice of "mission" in British Unitarian history. This will demonstrate how Unitarians have had a strong sense of mission in the past, but how the theological foundations for it have crumbled, leaving us concerned only with a pragmatic emphasis on "church growth". I will then begin to build an understanding of mission on the two foundations of a theology of revelation (the question of truth) and a theology of salvation (the question of faith). These two chapters are the most philosophically dense, and so if you, the reader, wish to skip over them to explore the more down-to-earth issues, then you can probably do so without losing the thread of my argument too much.

With those preliminaries out of the way, I will turn to the fundamental question of the purpose of Unitarianism. My answer to this question is that the Unitarian mission is both to discover and to create "paradise". I will explore what this spirituality of paradise might mean, and how it might provide a sense of vision and mission. With this overall mission in mind, I will then turn to the exploration of "evangelism" as a practice that Unitarians can carry out which draws us towards paradise. Evangelism is a powerful form of dialogue, and the last chapter of this book will give examples of how we can put this form of dialogue into practice in the life of individuals and congregations.

This is a work of practical theology, so I am attempting to be thoroughly theological and also thoroughly practical. My attempt here is to build both a language and a practice that will be useful for Unitarians, and indeed other religious liberals, in doing the work of religious community.

My understanding of the Unitarian tradition

Right at the outset I should make explicit my concept of the Unitarian tradition. My understanding is that it is just that – a tradition. Elsewhere I have argued that a tradition is a dynamic, evolving, human endeavour, and that the achievement of the moral life and the pursuit of truth is possible only by being part of a tradition.[6]

The Unitarian tradition is a specific historical set of stories, practices, institutions, attitudes, virtues, cultures, and writings. It is a progressive and liberal tradition, and so it allows for greater, and more rapid, evolution than many religious traditions, but that does not mean that it ceases to be a historical tradition. So although, for example, same-sex marriage was in no way part of the Unitarian tradition in the 1770s, today this practice can sit happily within it.[7]

What is equally true is that for most of its history Unitarian faith and theology involved an engagement with the stories of the Christian Bible. From the beginnings of explicit British Unitarianism in the 1770s until (perhaps?) the 1970s, attending a Unitarian church involved (among other things) engaging with the stories of the Bible. This is still true today in many, but not all, Unitarian congregations. That means that the language of Theophilus Lindsey, Joseph Priestley, Anna Laetitia Barbauld, Richard Wright, James Martineau, and other Unitarians of the past was a biblical language drawing on Christian theological categories and practices. Equally my work here to create a Unitarian understanding of mission draws upon biblical language. In other words, I am rooted in what I would call a "classical" understanding of the Unitarian tradition which sees the "fatherhood" (or parental loving nature) of God and the "leadership" of Jesus as important.

I am aware that not every contemporary British Unitarian will be able to go along with me in this commitment to "classical Unitarianism". Although, on paper, the General Assembly of Unitarian and Free Christian Churches has the aim of "upholding the liberal Christian tradition", in practice since the 1960s there has been a process of secularisation and post-modern fragmentation which has led to a rejection of much Christian language and practice. Some now would see Unitarianism as non-Christian, or post-Christian, or anti-Christian.

This is not my position. For me, if the word "Unitarian" is to have some kind of *consistent* meaning in the eighteenth, nineteenth, twentieth, and twenty-first centuries, then it must refer to something at least *rooted* in Christianity. To fully make this argument, however, would take another whole book, so for now I must simply state my position, rather than coherently argue for it. But it seems only fair and honest to say that my position is that classical Unitarianism is still a rich source of inspiration for thinking about these issues today.

This book is not an official document of the General Assembly of Unitarian and Free Christian Churches. It is the work of one single theologian and practitioner. Unitarians are of course free to disagree with its methods and conclusions. But I would humbly hope that even someone who strongly disagrees with much that I have written here will get something useful out of that disagreement. I hope that the path of my argument may offer something useful even to those people who may object to some or all of it. And I hope at least that readers will agree that the questions are urgent, even if different answers are offered. The theology that I am trying to develop here starts from the liberal, and ultimately agnostic, position that *we just don't know for sure*. My answers might be wrong. But I think that makes the process of struggling towards those answers even more urgent.

If this stimulates other writing that approaches things from a different perspective and strongly disagrees with my conclusions, then that is all to the good. Often it is by disagreeing with others that we can shape our own thoughts.

Who is this book for?

I have been trained in the traditions of contextual theology. That means that I take my own context seriously as my starting point in doing theology. My cultural context is British, and my theological context is Unitarian. I have taken British Unitarianism as my starting point in developing this theology. This book is primarily aimed at British Unitarians who wish to take the path of thinking deeply about these questions. It is a work of theology, and so its journey takes us down some fairly dense intellectual paths. I think these paths are worth taking, but I have tried to make things as clear and simple as possible, while also being intellectually rigorous. If I have failed to make my ideas as clear as they could be, then I ask for forgiveness and patience from the reader. My hope is that any intelligent, curious reader may derive something useful out of this, without being a specialist in theology.

I also hope that this book may be useful to Unitarian Universalists in North America, and other Unitarian communities around the world. Indeed, I believe it may also be useful to Quakers, liberal Christians, and other kinds of religious liberal. My starting point in this theology is the liberal sense that we do not have all the answers, that there is more mystery in the world than we know, and that it is impossible to make dogmatic claims that we are certain of the full and final truth. If you are committed to this kind of liberalism, but also wonder how your religious tradition can have a clear message to the world and a committed and enthusiastic sense of mission, then this book might be for you. If you have wondered how it might be possible to be both liberal and evangelical, then you are welcome to join me on this journey.

Questions for reflection and discussion

1. What would you say is the purpose of Unitarianism? How would you express it in your own words?

2. What is your initial reaction to the word "mission"? What associations does it have for you?

7

Endnotes

1   General Assembly of Unitarian and Free Christian Churches (2007), p.10.

2   Hunt (2004), p.28.

3   Hytch (2006), p. 47.

4   Hostler, in 1981, estimated the number of Unitarians in Britain at 15,000 (p.1). Seventeen years later Chryssides (p. 107) estimated the number to have halved to 7,000 plus 800 children. Surveying the Annual Reports each year suggests a membership of about 3,700 in 2006 (General Assembly of Unitarian and Free Christian Churches (2007), pp.39–40). By 2018 that number was about 2,900 (General Assembly of Unitarian and Free Christian Churches (2019), p.54).

5   Muir (2016), pp.3–4.

6   See Lingwood (2017), pp. 111–24.

7   I would argue that there were elements inherent in the tradition in the 1770s that allow for same-sex marriage to be a consistent evolution of the same tradition, but I will treat that argument as implicit for now.

1 "Mission" in Unitarian history

He sent me to give the good news to the poor,
Tell prisoners that they are prisoners no more,
Tell blind people that they can see,
And set the downtrodden free.

"God's Spirit is in my Heart": words by Alan T. Dale
(based on the Book of Isaiah)
(Hymn 262 in *Hymns of Faith and Freedom*)

In the summer of 2017 I was interviewed for the position of minister of Cardiff Unitarians/ Undodiaid Caerdydd. In my presentation to the committee I drew attention to their website, which mentioned that the Unitarian missionary Richard Wright visited Cardiff two hundred years ago. I told them, "One of my heroes is Richard Wright, and I think we're at a stage in history when we need to get back to that missionary work of two centuries ago."

Inspired by this history, I suggested that we shape a "pioneer ministry" in Cardiff. Missionary work in the twenty-first century must inevitably look different from missionary work in the nineteenth century. We probably wouldn't even want to call it "missionary work", but there is value in knowing our history when considering the issues of the present. Inspired by both Richard Wright and the nineteenth-century "domestic missions" (described below), I now work as a pioneer minister in Cardiff, creating an experimental, urban ministry beyond the walls of traditional church. Although my work looks to the future, it also looks to the past for inspiration.

In theory and in practice, we must look to the past to understand where we might be heading in the future. And so to begin our theological journey we must understand something of the history of a word like "mission", and how such a word has been used in history in general, and Unitarian history in particular.

Already in the Introduction I have used a cluster of terms: "mission", "evangelism", "church growth". Do these terms mean the same thing? Are they interchangeable? My initial answer is no, and the first part of the book is concerned with exploring and defining those terms within a liberal theology. Nevertheless, we need to start by defining our first term, "mission", in a broad and ecumenical sense. Terms like "evangelism" will come later.

What is mission? Defining it is a difficult task.[1] For much of Christian history the word "mission" was used in the context of Trinitarian theology to speak about such things as the *sending* of the Son by the Father.[2] In this sense the word has associations with the *actions of God*. Later, the Jesuits used the term "mission" to refer to the action of spreading the (Catholic) Christian faith among people who were not (Catholic) Christians.[3] In this sense mission has associations with the *actions of the Church*, specifically its expansion. These two motifs remain very relevant as we think about mission as something to do with the actions of God and the actions of a religious community, and something to do with how the two relate to each other.

It is worth keeping these two motifs in mind as we ask the question of how the word "mission" has been used in a Unitarian context. The word is in no way alien to the Unitarian tradition, so it is worth exploring what it has meant across Unitarian history.

What is most striking when surveying British Unitarian history on the lookout for the word "mission" is that it crops up a lot. The concept of "missionary activity" was taken up by Protestants later than it was by Catholics;[4] but, as the popularity of Protestant mission grew, it influenced Unitarians no less than any other group. If you look at the first generation of Unitarians, you see mission.

Despite this, the idea of mission or missionary activity is rarely dwelt upon in Unitarian historical surveys. Historians have generally dwelt on what Unitarians did and did not *believe*, and have largely ignored mission. But in fact there has been no era when "missionary" activity of some kind has been totally absent from Unitarian life. What "missionary" activity has been carried out by Unitarians, and what does that tell us about what "mission" might mean in a Unitarian context? What follows is far from an exhaustive study, but it presents a few historical vignettes to give some foundations for how we might think about Unitarian mission today.

Mission as preaching: Richard Wright

Unitarianism in Britain began in the age of the Enlightenment at the end of the eighteenth century. It originated not as a popular movement, but as a slow evolution towards liberalism among the intellectuals and ministers of already existing churches. Historically (and up to the present) it has often been questioned whether Unitarianism has any appeal to anyone except middle-class intellectuals.[5] And yet a counter-example to this culture is embodied at the very beginning of Unitarian history by Richard Wright (1764–1836). His vocation was as remarkable then as it would be today: he was a Unitarian missionary.[6]

Born of humble origins,[7] and growing up as a Baptist, by the age of nineteen Wright had rejected Calvinism[8] and soon embraced both universalism (a disbelief in eternal torment in hell) and unitarianism (a belief that the Father is the only God, and Jesus is purely human).[9] His theology was liberal, but his approach and style remained "Evangelical", and he took it upon himself, with a personal sense of missionary zeal, to spread the Unitarian gospel. He did so for many years without formal support,[10] but from 1806 onwards he was employed by the newly formed "Unitarian Fund for Promoting Unitarianism by means of Popular Preaching".

For the next twenty years Richard Wright was formally supported as a Unitarian missionary, walking and preaching across the country.[11] He described the work of the Fund (therefore also his own ministry) as "the universal diffusion of the pure doctrine and benignant spirit of the gospel, the general revival of primitive christianity [sic] both in faith and practice".[12] His belief was that Unitarianism was the original "primitive" Christianity – the pure gospel of Jesus Christ, "Christianity in its most simple and intelligible form"[13] without the addition of philosophical dogmas. It was the simple faith in the character of God as a loving father,[14] as taught by Jesus.

Two deep commitments guided his work:[15] one was that Unitarian Christianity was a faith that could appeal to the "poor and unlearned";[16] and the other was that the gospel could "make all men [sic] virtuous and happy"[17] – as opposed to Calvinism, which would lead to a meanness of spirit. It was a universal gospel, so it should be available to all people, rich and poor, north and south.

And so Richard Wright walked from village to village, from town to town, and he preached. He preached, it seems, in every Unitarian congregation that existed in Britain at the time. He preached in the open air, in hired rooms, or in sympathetic chapels and meeting houses.[18] That he made such journeys to every corner of Great Britain, from Scotland to Cornwall, before the age of the railways is quite remarkable. It is also remarkable that when he began, Unitarianism was technically illegal, and in theory he could have been arrested in England, and even executed in Scotland, for spreading Unitarian Christianity.[19]

Wright preached largely to the rural poor. He worked entirely within a "Christendom" context, where it was assumed that everyone was basically already Christian to some degree, and so the issue of people of different religious traditions was not relevant to his work. However, he did state that "christianity [sic] is designed to be universal, it is destined to be the religion of the whole world", although this was in the context of arguing that Unitarianism was for the working classes as well as the educated classes.[20] Wright never engaged with non-Christians; however, he did support foreign missions,[21] and we can ascertain from his writings that he did believe in the superiority of Christianity to other religions.

Wright clearly believed in a missionary God, a God of purpose. He believed he had been commissioned by God to be a missionary, and that even his physical body had been providentially designed for the work of a walking evangelist.[22] He believed that what he was doing was God's work; he wrote of "God's gracious plans"[23] and of "what he hath done by me".[24]

Wright's missionary enthusiasm was rare for Unitarians in the early nineteenth century, and it remained rare throughout the century. There is a sense in his writings at the end of his career that he sincerely wished for a new generation of Unitarian missionaries to succeed him. But it was not to be. Unitarianism remained largely lukewarm and middle class. It is interesting to speculate how things might have been different if Wright's enthusiastic evangelistic style had become more dominant and shaped the denomination after his time. In many ways Wright's style was more Universalist than Unitarian. There was a smattering of Universalist churches around at the time, and Wright had friendly connections with them.[25] But they never became a strong denomination in Britain as they did in the United States of America. In the United States the Universalists tended to come from the Baptists, and, like Richard Wright, tended to be of a lower social class, less well educated, and preferring extemporaneous preaching (rather than a well-educated minister delivering a written sermon, as was the Unitarian tradition).[26] Although our subject here is primarily the British tradition, it is worth mentioning the American Universalists because, despite, by definition, believing that everyone will be saved, their style and tradition remained evangelistic. Like the Methodists, on the American "frontier" the Universalist preachers were circuit riders, braving all weathers on horseback, and going from place to place to preach the gospel.[27] They were truly evangelical liberals.[28]

Mission as urban social work: the domestic missions

After Richard Wright the word "mission" in a British Unitarian context seems to have travelled in a different direction. As the nineteenth century wore on, the industrial revolution was transforming British society, and cities and towns were growing exponentially, drawing in workers from rural areas to the new factories and industries. This created new social problems for the new urban poor, who suffered under the strains of poverty and inadequate housing, and had few civil or political rights. In Boston, Massachusetts, the Unitarian minister Joseph Tuckerman had responded to similar problems by setting up a "domestic mission". In 1834 he toured England speaking about his work, and the response was that a number of British domestic missions were set up by Unitarians in large cities and towns in the next few years.[29]

This was mission aimed at the poor, as it was for Richard Wright. The missionaries, recognising that most of the urban poor population did not go to church, launched an evangelistic ministry "preaching good news to the poor". However, the domestic missionaries soon realised that they could not deal solely with religious issues while ignoring the social problems. This is exemplified by a woman who is reported to have said to the domestic missionary in Liverpool, "You see, Sir, when you've no meat, it puts thought of going to a place of worship out of your mind."[30]

The domestic missions therefore emphasised not only bringing the gospel to the poor, but also helping them to cope with social, financial, and personal problems.[31] This was also a ministry that had some concern for structural issues and campaigned for the reform of certain laws.[32] The "Minister to the Poor" visited homes to encourage piety, but also offered help in practical ways. Eventually this led to the establishment of Sunday Schools, adult educational facilities,[33] and new places of worship.[34] There was certainly a paternalistic and patronising dimension to middle-class aspirations to "improve" the working classes. However, there is no doubt that the motives were honourable, and that much good work was carried out. The first minister of the Liverpool Domestic Mission, John Johns, even died of typhoid fever, contracted while carrying out his duties, a Unitarian martyr to this ministry,[35] though today entirely forgotten. What does it mean, I wonder, that today Unitarians remember those heretics executed for their religious beliefs, but have forgotten those Unitarians who died serving the poor?

The ministry of the domestic missions was understood as the religious and moral improvement of the poor. The variety of the ministry on offer certainly seems to suggest that there was a very holistic understanding of mission. The social problems encountered included alcoholism, bad housing, bad sanitation, and lack of education. The missions did their best to address all of these problems.

The task of Ministers to the Poor was to encourage "religion" and "worship" among those with whom they worked, but there was also an attempt to avoid being sectarian (although it was Christian religion that was being encouraged). This description from a Manchester Domestic Mission report is worth quoting in full:

. . . the Minister to the Poor is not sent among them in a sectarian character. His mission is to those who are not connected with any religious society; and his business is, if possible, to awaken attention to religion and to recommend attendance upon public worship without having in view the interests of any particular sect. But they [the subscribers] must also be aware that it cannot be required of him to conceal his particular opinions, or to pretend less value for them than he actually feels.[36]

In theory at least, the gospel preached was a religious (Christian) one, preached to the unchurched poor, but without the belief of Richard Wright that primitive (Unitarian) Christianity was the only Christianity worth preaching and practising. There was a more ecumenical spirit to this mission, although there was still an assumption that it was best to practise "simple" Christianity. As one of the supporters of the Liverpool Mission put it, they were preaching and practising "the Christianity of the Sermon on the Mount, of the Lord's Prayer, of the parable of the Prodigal Son; the Christianity of the life of Christ".[37]

This demonstrates a tension that has existed throughout Unitarian history around the question of whether Unitarians wanted to promote their own particular tradition, or whether as pluralists and ecumenists they should be promoting Christianity in general, or (later) religion in general, or (later still) liberalism in general.

Theologically, I have found no direct reference to the work being seen as the "will of God", although it seems likely that this idea would not have been refuted. The inaugural meeting of the Liverpool Domestic Mission in 1837 contained this declaration: "That Christianity, in declaring the equal relation of all men [sic] to the Universal Parent, imposes an obligation on its professors by extending its influence to the most destitute, to equalize, as far as may be, the moral condition of all His children".[38]

There was a sense that following Jesus necessarily led to a concern for the poor. George Buckland, Minister to the Poor in Manchester, wrote in 1839, "our duty as individuals is obvious; as professed disciples of Jesus Christ, we have but one course to pursue, that of doing good to the uttermost of our power".[39]

It is worth noting what seems to be a blind spot in this work. It could be argued that the Christian work of "equalising" all God's children should require a response from the rich rather than the poor. Perhaps it was the rich and comfortable who needed to respond to the gospel, to address the structures of society that led to such suffering for the poor. Perhaps it was the rich who really needed conversion, rather than the poor. Such thinking was not present in the work of the domestic missions. This was philanthropy, not revolution. Nevertheless, one vocal supporter of the missions did reflect that there was an "even more difficult work" than that of the domestic missions to the poor, and this was "inspiring with the spirit of Christianity those in whom prosperity and comfort have produced indifference and selfishness".[40]

The domestic missions continued in some form until the twentieth century, although much of the work of education, health care, and social care began to be taken up by the state.[41] Eventually the practice of employing a "Minister to the Poor" ceased, and the work gradually became small-scale social work, rather than ambitious religious mission.

In the second half of the nineteenth century the baton of missionary work begun by the domestic missions was arguably taken on by the founders of the Unitarian Home Missionary Board in 1854. The Board was established to train Unitarian ministers able to serve the urban poor. The national 1851 Religious Census revealed low levels of church attendance among the urban working classes, and this served as a major impetus for the creation of the Board.[42] The impetus was one of service, but it was also explicitly evangelical, and explicitly evangelical for Unitarianism. John Relly Beard (1800–1876) said of the mission of the Board, "Ours is essentially an aggressive attitude: ... we go forth as avowed Unitarians, hoping, with the blessing of God, to found, restore and replenish Unitarian Churches".[43] The Board evolved into the Home Missionary College in 1889, only dropping the label "missionary" in 1926 and becoming simply Unitarian College Manchester.[44]

Nineteenth-century Unitarian missionary zeal led to the founding of a number of churches, most often daughter churches from existing congregations, and often planted in areas of greater poverty. Many of these congregations were successful, and many continue to this day. Today the echoes of this missionary attitude are preserved in the name of certain Unitarian regional districts which still include the word "mission" in their titles.

Mission as converting non-Christians: the Unitarian mission in India

In common usage, words like "mission" and "missionary" conjure up the idea of *foreign* mission: the image from the Victorian era of a white Christian missionary (perhaps backed up by colonial power) preaching Christianity to non-Christians in Africa or Asia or the Americas. This image is strongly condemned by today's Western liberals, who perceive it as imperialistic, coercive, and intolerant. This is perhaps a caricature, and although Western missionaries were sometimes involved in horrendous acts of violence and coercion, the whole history is more nuanced than this, and often involved missionaries resisting the violence of imperial power.[45]

Nevertheless, with this image in mind, contemporary Unitarians may be surprised to learn that Unitarians did indeed engage in foreign missionary activity, though never on a grand scale, and always with a degree of uncertainty. The story of Unitarian mission in India is a fascinating one. It began with William Adam (1796–1881), a British Baptist missionary in Calcutta. While working on a translation of the New Testament into Bengali, with a Brahmin called Rammohun Roy (1772–1833), Adam rejected the doctrine of the Trinity and became a Unitarian.[46] It was as a result of dialogue with a Hindu that Adam converted from a Baptist faith to a Unitarian one! This is typical of the intertwined relationship between Unitarianism and the Brahmo Samaj, the liberal Hindu reform movement founded by Roy some years later.

Roy was at first very interested in Unitarianism, and in 1821 Adam, Roy, and other Calcutta Brahmins formed the Calcutta Unitarian Committee, with a largely educational purpose of spreading knowledge about "the religion of Christ".[47] The idea was that this should start by spreading the message first to the local European population and subsequently to the native Indian population, mainly the Brahmins.[48] By 1822 Unitarian services were being held in a rented house, led by Adam.[49] Adam wrote to British Unitarians in 1822, and later to American Unitarians, proposing a large-scale missionary project.[50] But financial support by both American and British Unitarians for such a scheme was always lukewarm at best.[51]

By 1828 Roy aspired to create a decidedly more Hindu organisation, and he formed the Brahmo Samaj, or Society of God, as a liberal and monotheistic form of Hinduism. From then on the liberally minded Brahmins of Calcutta began to put their energy into a religious community that was more Hindu than Christian.[52] Adam's mission struggled. Nevertheless the Brahmo Samaj maintained warm relations with British Unitarians – as shown by the fact that Roy was staying with Unitarian friends in Bristol when he died in 1833.

In 1855 a new missionary effort was launched by American Unitarians, who sent Charles Dall (1816–1886) as Unitarian missionary to Calcutta.[53] His instructions read as follows: "You go out as a Unitarian missionary because we have reason to believe that many will receive the gospel as we hold it... But you are not expected to carry mere doctrinal discussions and sectarian strifes to those distant lands."[54]

Dall maintained strong relations with the Brahmo Samaj and distributed the works of famous Unitarian ministers among its members.[55] He founded educational institutions, distributed leaflets, and established a mission station. Although some were interested in Unitarian Christianity,[56] and he met with Indian Christians who had become anti-Trinitarians,[57] in the long term Dall's mission was not much more successful than Adam's. Clearly many Indians were interested in (Unitarian) Christianity, but very few of them were prepared to give up their Hindu or Brahmo identity.[58]

To persuade these members of the Brahmo Samaj to take the step into Unitarian Christianity, Dall took the radical step of becoming a member of the Brahmo Samaj.[59] It is debatable, and was debated,[60] whether Unitarian Christianity was theologically compatible with Brahmo Samaj Hinduism. The Brahmo Samaj itself at that time was undergoing considerable evolution under the leadership of Keshub Chunder Sen. The Brahmos began to see themselves as following "Absolute Religion" beyond any sectarianism:[61] a universalistic theism following all "great men"[62] (sic).

They began to see Roy's interest in Jesus as unnecessary.[63] Sen did not see Brahmoism as a bridge to Unitarian Christianity as Dall did, but rather saw Christianity as a bridge to Brahmoism![64] It is worth noting, however, that Unitarianism itself was beginning to take the first few steps down the same theological path, and worth considering whether it may be a "universal religion" beyond adherence to Christianity.

Caste always played a large part in the missions in Calcutta. They were always aimed at the higher-caste Indians. However, the Brahmins were reluctant to convert to Christianity for fear of being associated with outcast converts,[65] although many of the more liberal-minded of them were prepared to become members of the Brahmo Samaj. The mission to win high-caste Unitarian Christians was never successful. It is perhaps worth noting that the only successful Unitarian Christian communities consisted of lower-caste Indians, and were initiated and led by Indians, rather than planted from foreign missions: the Unitarian Christian Church of Chennai (Madras) and the Khasi Unitarian Union in North East India. The histories of these communities are quite different.

The missions to Calcutta did not result in a large number of Indians becoming Unitarians, but arguably they did result in (or at least encourage) the growth of the Brahmo Samaj, which maintains good relations with the Unitarian community to this day. The missionary work in India began to confront Unitarians with the reality of pluralism and began a path that would see Unitarians increasingly valuing truth and salvation that could come from other faiths. This can be seen in the Unitarians who began to reflect theologically on what it meant to do mission in India. Dall himself spoke of the mission as learning and doing the will of God,[66] but other theological reflections came from American supporters of the mission.[67] Joseph Tuckerman, pioneer of domestic mission in Boston, also supported foreign missions, but he recognised the Unitarian reluctance to engage in mission and linked it directly to the fact that Unitarians believed that anyone could be saved, regardless of whether or not they were Christian. He still insisted that religious "bigotry" was worth fighting against, however, whether it came from "Calvinism" or the "Brahmanical faith".[68] William Ellery Channing, the most important Unitarian theologian at the time, offered a critique of missions by stressing the universal nature of God's laws and love which are available to all;[69] nevertheless, he did support the Indian mission of William Adam.

Although Adam was strongly outspoken in his campaigning on a number of social-justice issues in India, this seems to have been a function of his other capacities, such as journalism, rather than an integral part of his ministry and mission.[70] Dall too was deeply involved in social issues, perhaps as a more integrated part of his mission. However, the "traditional" sense of mission, that of converting people to Christianity, remained the ideal aim for both of them, though they were clearly supportive of more liberal, more Christian-like, movements in Hinduism.

Adam's deep sympathy and friendship with Rammohun Roy could suggest that the doctrines of the Brahmo Samaj were acceptable to him. Thus one could argue that the gospel preached was rational liberal monotheism, and whether that came in Christian or Hindu form mattered little.[71] Joseph Tuckerman wrote that Roy was "in the spirit of Christianity", and that this mattered more than whether he explicitly identified as Christian.[72] Charles Dall wrote that "Christianity is ... God's truth and God's love embodied in human life";[73] however, God's truth had also come to other people in other times.[74] He did support the Brahmo Samaj and clearly thought it was an improvement on "superstitious" Hinduism.

Many years later, in 1913, the American Unitarian minister, Jabez T. Sunderland, wrote a definition of Unitarian mission that seems to state that explicit Christianity is unnecessary:

> Our wish is to carry to non-Christian peoples a form of Christianity
> which is world-wide in its sympathies ... We go not to destroy
> such venerable historical religions as Buddhism, Hinduism,
> Confucianism or even Mohammedism [sic], but to assist such of
> their followers to improve them, to purify them, to reform them, to
> let shine upon them the light of modern knowledge, and thus purge
> away their superstitions and their lower elements, and lift them up
> to the level of their own best teachings.[75]

Although potentially imperialistic and patronising, these sentiments do represent the first steps towards a fuller embrace of a theology of pluralism that Unitarians would adopt in the twentieth century. As Unitarians became more aware of pluralism and appreciated the spiritual riches of other religions, the concept of "mission" became less and less meaningful.

Mission as preaching (again): the Van Mission

In Britain in the twentieth century there was one last "hurrah" for classic Unitarian "missionary work" – and that was the Van Mission. In 1907, Thomas P. Spedding and Bertram Talbot took up permanent positions as Unitarian missionaries, engaged in open-air preaching, supported by a horse-drawn van. Beginning with one van, by the end of the venture there were six on the road.[76] A van would draw into a town, and in the evening a preacher would preach the Unitarian message for up to an hour to anyone who would listen[77] – and clearly many hundreds did.[78] The aim of the Van Mission was to proclaim the Unitarian message. The preachers' intention did not seem to be directly to plant churches or gain converts, but to state their faith, and abide by the consequences.[79] Many people were in agreement with the message preached to them, but without any new congregations to take the next step the mission had little success in the long term.[80]

The stated object of the Van Mission was to "spread a knowledge of Unitarian principles in villages and districts where no churches of our faith exist, and to co-operate with existing churches, missionary associations and the Postal Missions, wherever possible".[81] There was a sense that the Unitarian message was a positive one which needed to be heard: "It is felt that on the living questions of the hour Unitarians have a message of courage and cheer which should be spoken".[82] The preacher did not say "only believe and you will be saved", but appealed to his listeners' "own reason and every-day experience", saying "we ask you to listen to what we have to say, and then leave it to you for what it's worth".[83] This was an attempt at evangelism that was not coercive or over-aggressive.

The message was preached to whomever happened to stop by and listen. However, there was no doubt an element of social class in this venture: as one commentator wrote, initiating the Van Mission was a task of breaking "through the fence of 'respectability'", contrasting the preaching to crowds in the open air with "a mere handful of unresponsive but dignified hearers" in existing congregations.[84]

The Van Mission seemed to have little theology underpinning it. The missionaries clearly believed that the Unitarian message was worth proclaiming, but there is little sense that they were fulfilling God's purposes in this mission. As the twentieth century wore on, this work continued in the form of "postal missions" (founded in 1866) and later the National Unitarian Fellowship (founded in 1944). As the Unitarian denomination finally organised itself in the twentieth century into the current General Assembly of Unitarian and Free Christian Churches, much of the work of "promoting Unitarianism" was undertaken by such structures in producing books and leaflets, and, later, using the internet.

Mission as church growth: the late twentieth-century development

The twentieth century witnessed a serious decline in Unitarian numbers. This of course did not go unnoticed, and there have been those who have occasionally sought ways to reverse the decline. However, a tension has always existed between a desire for growth and Unitarianism's liberal theology. Nevertheless, in the face of twentieth-century decline, many Unitarians have become more explicit about actively seeking church growth. In doing so, many have inevitably turned to ideas and books about the subject of church growth, seeking to apply the same principles but without assuming the theology of mainstream or conservative Christian authors.

This "church growth movement" is distinguished from all other forms of Unitarian mission that we have hitherto surveyed in its approach to mission as *"come to us"*, rather than *"go to them"*. There is not a sense of going where the people are, where the unchurched, or the poor, or the foreigners are, but rather asking them to come to us. It is not a movement of the confident church going out, but the declining church seeking to ensure its own health and survival.

Nevertheless, initially in the United States, and subsequently in Great Britain, many Unitarians have been more open to the idea of church growth and have even synonymously used the word "evangelism". In 1994

American Unitarian Universalists published *Salted with Fire,* in which the editor, Scott Alexander, writes that scores "of Unitarian Universalist leaders (both clergy and laity) are talking openly and enthusiastically about evangelism"[85] and that the book contains essays by "a group of unashamedly evangelistic Unitarian Universalist leaders".[86] There is a sense in this book, and in others subsequently, that there is something very valuable in the Unitarian Universalist community, and that Unitarian Universalists should not be ashamed to say this and promote themselves. One of the writers, Lawrence Peers, writes of often hearing the refrain "If only I had known about Unitarian Universalism sooner …".[87]

The situation in North America is, of course, rather different from that in Great Britain. Religious decline has not hit as seriously and deeply in North America as it has here. There are huge differences, as well as important similarities, between the two cultures. Equally there are important differences, as well as significant similarities, between American Unitarian Universalism and British Unitarianism. We don't need to explore those differences in depth, but for our current purposes it is worth noting the influence of American Unitarian Universalism on British Unitarianism. In a globalised, digital age, it is of course equally easy to access US websites and British ones; so when two nations share the same language, there is of course going to be some influence. Not only that, but there has been a steady stream of American ministers serving the British denomination. My impression is that this has been a not insignificant influence in bringing American ideas of "church growth" into British Unitarianism.

In my judgement I would say that the ideas of church growth have been effective in a smattering of congregations, who have grown, or at least held steady in membership numbers. But this has not reversed the overall trend of decline across the denomination. And so we return to our starting point of the 2006 resolution which simply says "in order to survive we must grow".

But why? This new enthusiasm for church growth has been very inarticulate in its failure to present a clear message or reflect theologically on the nature of the message. The emphasis in writing on church growth in the last thirty years has been more practical than theological. For example, the chapter contributed by the American Terasa Cooley in *Why Liberal*

Churches Are Growing contains no theological reflection on the justification or motivation for growth, but only mentions in passing things like the use of "God language"[88] and spiritual topics in preaching.[89] Similarly, in an Irish context Bill Darlison's essay in *Prospects for the Unitarian Movement* (2002) offers practical tips for growth (although they are certainly religiously informed), but it is not in itself a religious or theological reflection on growth. In a British context we have John Midgley's *The Growing Edge* (1996), in which the author reflects on six years as national Development Officer for the denomination, but again it is light on theology.[90]

If there is any kind of philosophy behind contemporary Unitarian thinking on church growth, it is a kind of liberal optimism. There is a sense that on a number of issues, such as gay rights, and broad tolerance of other religions, Unitarians are more in line with general British culture than is mainstream Christianity. So the argument goes that "lots of people would come to us if only they knew about us, if only we were better at getting the message out". This is asserted more often than argued, and whether or not it is actually true is a question that deserves some attention. If Unitarians had an infinite publicity budget and could invest millions in "getting our message out", would this result in growth, or might that depend on what exactly "the message" was? What is the message?

The problem is that "the message" has become less and less clear. Whereas throughout the nineteenth century, and into most of the twentieth century, Unitarian faith could be fairly summarised as belief in the fatherhood of one God, the "brotherhood of man", and the leadership of a human Jesus,[91] in contemporary times the message is not so simple. There has been a gradual shift away from Christian language and practice and into a post-modern liberalism that has been characterised (some would say unfairly) as "you can believe anything you want". This makes it increasingly difficult, in the work of promotion and church growth, to explain Unitarianism and make it clear *what* we are inviting someone into.

This is a problem that will be explored throughout this book. For now, let us simply note the glaring "why" question, the theological question, that hangs over all of this. The nearest thing to an in-depth theological reflection on mission in a British Unitarian context in recent times is the writing of Cathal Courtney. His *Towards Beloved Community* (2007), based on talks at a Unitarian Summer School, is an exploration of post-modernity, community, and the individual, and it deals with many of the same issues that we will touch on here. In another essay he explicitly rejects a concentration on numbers and offers a transcending purpose for the Unitarian community: what he calls the transfiguration of life.[92] This is one of the few attempts to offer a theological and spiritual self-transcending purpose for Unitarianism other than the sense that "we must grow to survive".

What can we learn from history?

There are many themes running through this brief survey of the history of Unitarian mission. There have always been tensions around the question of whether Unitarians were promoting their own particular faith/denomination or whether they wanted to work in a non-sectarian or ecumenical (or eventually interfaith) manner.

Similarly, there have always been tensions around issues of social class, race, power, privilege, and imperialism. Although Unitarians are perhaps less guilty than other Christians of racism and colonialism in their approach to foreign missions, the reality of white privilege and power in the age of the British Empire should not be ignored. But on British soil too there were always issues of class and economic privilege. In mission there is always the danger of the more powerful and privileged doing mission *to* those with less power and privilege. It can be (and often was) a paternalistic and disempowering activity.

However, we must also recognise that *not* doing mission can also be an expression of class prejudice and racism. There can be an attitude of "we don't want those people in our churches". A reluctance to reach out to others in mission may be a fear of "the other" and a desire to keep our church white and middle class. Such realities and tensions have never been absent from Unitarian history.

All of the above are important issues. But I would like to end here by considering the theological issues, which will lead us into the next chapters. Across Unitarian missionary history we have seen a decline in the confidence with which Unitarians were certain that they were following the will of God in mission. Richard Wright spoke freely of a providential God who guided his work, and he spoke of himself as "merely an instrument in the hands of that great Being".[93] That confidence petered away over the centuries, as Unitarians spoke less about God and more about Unitarianism itself.

Parallel with this development was a declining confidence in the belief that Unitarians were the primary possessors of truth and salvation. The Unitarian mission in India represented an encounter with the full life and complexity of another religious tradition. Those encounters have continued through the years in multiple ways. Different religions have deeply influenced contemporary Unitarian practice, and in some ways have been incorporated into Unitarianism itself. Some would even argue that today Unitarianism is a "universalistic" or "pan-religionist" movement.[94]

All of this has distanced Unitarianism further and further from mainstream Christian thinking about mission. This has led us to a place where Unitarians want to promote their religion but have no language for doing so. Unitarians want to grow – but can't say why. And so the word "mission" has had less and less meaning.

The "why" question still hangs over us. We must begin to try to answer it. We will begin by offering two possible answers which might seem to work from a mainstream Christian perspective, and see how they can be applied to a Unitarian context. One answer could be "because we have the truth". Another answer could be "because this is the way of salvation". Both answers are deeply problematic from a liberal perspective – but we need to delve deeper into why and how they are problematic, and ask what might be left when we deal with those problems.

Questions for reflection and discussion

1. What role has preaching played in your Unitarian journey? Has it had a significant transformative effect in your spiritual / religious life?

2. What is your current sense of "the message" of Unitarianism as you have internalised it (i.e. without going and looking it up)?

3. Can you think of alternative means by which we Unitarians could "preach" to the wider world in order to spread our message in the twenty-first century?

4. Are you surprised to learn that Unitarians did foreign missionary work? What issues does this bring up for you?

Endnotes

1   Bosch (1991), pp.511–12.

2   Bosch (1991), p.1.

3   Bosch (1991), p.1.

4   Bosch (1991), p. 245.

5   Howe (1997), p.159.

6   McLachlan (1998) writes that he was "a rara avis, the only missionary in Unitarian history" (p.vi); but this is incorrect, as we shall see.

7   McLachlan (1998), p.2.

8   McLachlan (1998), p.5.

9   McLachlan (1998), p.7. The lower case here is deliberate, to indicate a theological belief rather than a denomination. Wright came to these beliefs before he belonged in an official sense to the Unitarian denomination, and there were only a handful of self-proclaimed "Universalist" churches in Britain at that time.

10   Wright (1824), pp.70–71.

11   McLachlan (1998), p.11.

12   Wright (1824), p.iv.

13   This phrase is used in the trust deed of the Hibbert Trust; see Brown (2006), p.1.

14   Wright (1824), p.357.

15   McLachlan (1998), p.15.

16   Wright (1824), p.viii.

17   Wright (1824), p. 26.

18   McLachlan (1998), p.20.

19   Wright (1824), p.ix.

20   Wright (1824), p.30.

21   Wright (1824), p.91.

22   McLachlan (1998), p.31.

23   Wright (1824), p.xi.

24   Wright (1824), p.13.

25 Wright (1824), p.286.

26 Cassara (1997), p.5.

27 Cassara (1997), p.126.

28 In 1961 the Universalists merged with the Unitarians, as the two traditions were always very similar, and today the American denomination is known as the Unitarian Universalist Association.

29 Holt (1936), pp.11–12.

30 Holt (1936), p.60.

31 Perry (1933), pp.7–8.

32 Perry (1933), pp.4, 12.

33 Perry (1933), p.11.

34 Perry (1933), pp.6 and 12.

35 Holt (1936), p.48.

36 Perry (1933), p.7.

37 J.H. Thom, as quoted in Holt (1936), p.90. What was never appreciated in such theologies was that it is impossible not to be sectarian. This vision may be of a "minimalistic" Christianity, but to argue that this is the best type of Christianity is to argue against the majority branches of Christianity (Catholicism and Orthodoxy). It is not a neutral position. This is why, philosophically, the concept of "Free Christianity" is seriously flawed.

38 Holt (1936), p.88.

39 Perry (1933), p.15.

40 Holt (1936), p.85.

41 Holt (1936), p.104.

42 Smith, L. (2004), pp.53–5.

43 Quoted in Smith, L. (2004), p.55.

44 Smith, L. (2004), p.75.

45 Thiessen (2011), pp.98–103.

46 Lavan (1977), p.41.

47 Lavan (1977), pp.57–8.

48 Lavan (1977), p.51.

49 Lavan (1977), p.58.

50 Lavan (1977), p.62.

51 Lavan (1977), pp.63–4.

52 Lavan (1977), p.69.

53 Lavan (1977), p.82.

54 Quoted in Seaburg (1994), p.54.

55 Lavan (1977), p.86.

56 Dall (1857, p.15) reports that in eleven months 145 men came to the Mission Room to find out about Christianity.

57 He had conversations with some native Indian missionaries trained by Trinitarian Christians who had suffered in loss of support after rejecting the Trinity (Dall, pp.16–18).

58 Lavan (1977), pp.102–3.

59 Lavan (1977), p.122.

60 Lavan (1977), pp.122–3.

61 Lavan (1977), p.110.

62 Lavan (1977), p.113.

63 Dall (1857), p.33.

64 Lavan (1977), p.110.

65 Lavan (1977), p.67.

66 Dall (1857), p.20.

67 Lavan (1977), pp.94–7.

68 Lavan (1977), p.64.

69 Lavan (1977), p.65.

70 Lavan (1977), pp.46–51, 53–5.

71   Adam said that the Unity of God was central to Roy's theology (Lavan, 1977, pp.52–3).

72   Lavan (1977), p.66.

73   Lavan (1977), p.88.

74   Lavan (1977), p.88.

75   Lavan (1977), p.168.

76   Roberts (1978), p.193, note 1.

77   Roberts (1978), p.189.

78   Roberts (1978), p.190.

79   Roberts (1978), p.189.

80   Roberts (1978), p.192.

81   Roberts (1978), p.188.

82   Roberts (1978), p.188.

83   Roberts (1978), p.189.

84   Roberts (1978), p.191.

85   Alexander (1994), p.2.

86   Alexander (1994), p.5.

87   Peers (1994), p.63.

88   Cooley (2006), p.67.

89   Cooley (2006), p.66.

90   In this context "development" refers to the development of congregations so that they become healthy and growing.

91   See Clarke (1886).

92   Courtney (2002), p.70.

93   Wright (1824), p.13.

94   Marshall (2007), p.1.

2 Revelation and the search for truth

God, that word abideth ever;
Revelation is not sealed.

"God of Ages and of Nations"; words by Samuel Longfellow
(Hymn 75 in *Hymns for Living*)

How can we know the will of God?

Market Street in Manchester is probably the busiest pedestrianised street in the city. Anyone getting off a bus in Piccadilly Gardens and walking towards the Arndale Shopping Centre, or to many other areas in the city, is forced to go through this squashed mass of people. As such it is always full of beggars, buskers, little market stalls, and also evangelists.

Walking through this throng one Saturday, I noted that I could have been "evangelised" by Evangelical Christians, Muslims, and Jehovah's Witnesses, all within a few feet from each other. Of course, like most people on a busy Saturday afternoon, I avoided all of them and went on to do my shopping. But if I had stopped and talked to all of them, each would have claimed to tell me the truth, each would have claimed to be following God's will, each would have claimed to be fulfilling the mission of God by leading people towards the one true faith.

Is one of them right? Or are they all right? Or are they all wrong? Would I want to set myself up as someone with yet another rival truth in this literal market place of ideas? If Richard Wright were alive today, is that what he would be doing?

Maybe, but we do not live in the same world as Richard Wright – in terms of either theology or culture. Unitarian theology is not in the same place as it was two hundred years ago. If we look to the Unitarian missionary theology of Wright (considered in the previous chapter), we can see that it was founded on a number of assertions:

- that "mission" meant the promotion of Christian faith, the preaching of the Christian gospel;
- that Unitarian Christianity was the simplest, most "primitive", and therefore best form of Christianity;
- that, although all people will be reconciled to God (saved) eventually (no one is going eternally to hell), Christianity is still the truest and best faith that will make all people most happy and fulfilled;
- that a personal God desired this message to be preached to all, and that God called missionaries to this work.

Through the years we have seen that Unitarians have had less and less confidence in all these assertions. In fact, like many in this age that some call "post-modern", Unitarians are sceptical of any and all claims to truth. When there are so many rival claims to truth, how can we possibly know which is truly true? Or in some sense are they all true? Or is none of them true?

Truth is a more complicated business for us than it was for Richard Wright. What is the truth? How do we find out? What do we know? And how do we know it? Such questions are important if we are going to ask questions about mission. One common-usage definition of mission might be "the promotion of truth". But what truth? The Christian theologian tends to answer "the truth of the gospel of Jesus Christ, the truth of the purpose of a purposeful God". Christian theologians of mission, known as missiologists, tend to start from this sort of assertion, and then build their theology from there.

For example, J. Andrew Kirk writes about the theology of (Christian) mission as "a disciplined study which deals with questions that arise when people of faith seek to understand and fulfil God's purposes in the world, as these are demonstrated in the ministry of Jesus Christ".[1] This is an example of the idea of *missio Dei* – the mission of God. This idea has become the dominant theology in all mainstream Christian thinking about mission. The idea is that mission is not (primarily) about the actions of people or the expansion of the church, but is primarily about what God is doing. Mission is a movement from God towards the world, and the church is an instrument for that mission. These are the ideas that have dominated mainstream Trinitarian theology about mission for the past one hundred years.[2]

But this theology ignores a vital question: *how do you know* God's mission? How do you know that God's purposes are demonstrated most fully in the ministry of Jesus Christ? How do you know, for example, that God's purposes aren't revealed in the incorruptible revelation given directly to the Prophet Muhammad? Christian missiology tends to ignore these questions and gets on with exploring how to follow God's mission revealed in Jesus Christ.[3] But this seems to me to be a little intellectually dishonest. How can you ignore the most vital questions of all – how do you know what you know? How can you know the will of God? How can you know about God at all?

Charles Dall went to India as a Unitarian missionary with the idea of spreading Unitarian Christianity. But while there, his encounter with Hinduism changed him. He encountered something of God, something of truth, in those whom he met, and, as we have seen, he eventually joined the Brahmo Samaj (while remaining a Unitarian). In the process of his missionary work he discovered the truth, not only in his own position, but in those he encountered. To him at least, it seemed that there was truth in both Christianity and Hinduism. He thought he knew the truth of God (in Christianity), but then discovered something of the truth of God in Hinduism.

This story demonstrates something of the Unitarian attitude since then, which has been an openness to discovering truth, discovering God, in other religious traditions. What does this imply about a Unitarian approach to the question of the will of God, the mission of God, the truth of God, and how we know it? What does it imply about what we might call "revelation" – the way in which we know about God?

The question of God

Before we can explore the subject of revelation, we must first, briefly, explore the more foundational subject of God. Although it is tempting to fudge the issue and leave things in a liberal vague language that will allow for different interpretations, for the sake of honesty I think we have to tackle the question of God head-on. The main reason why the language of "the mission of God" may not work for some contemporary Unitarians is the simple fact that they don't believe in God.

In the twentieth century Unitarianism began to define itself more by the *process* of free enquiry than by the beliefs that had generally resulted from that process (the oneness of God, the humanity of Jesus, etc.). Within a liberal openness to new ideas, some began to advocate a non-theistic humanism. While this position has never been totally dominant, its inclusion of course involves a faith where God is no longer in the centre, but is optional. The most significant visible shift in theology was perhaps the publication of *Hymns for Living* in 1985. This replaced *Hymns of Worship: Revised,* last published in 1962. Comparing these two hymn books, we can see a shift from worship that explicitly and unapologetically worshipped God to one where many hymns did not mention God but rather praised liberal values.[4]

As I say, it is tempting to continue to use a vague liberal language in an attempt to avoid conflict and disagreement. However, I believe that it is more honest for me to simply state now that the theological project that I am trying to build here cannot continue if the idea of God is rejected entirely. It is impossible to do so while remaining committed to classical Unitarianism.

Thus we are continuing on this journey from a position of liberal agnosticism, from an attitude of *openness* to the possibility of transcendence.[5] That does not settle the question of God: quite the opposite. We are still just beginning. But it seems that at this stage it is important to be clear that we are operating with an openness to the possibility of transcendence, with an openness to the possibility that the symbol "God" points to something worth considering, and something rooted in what the Unitarian tradition has taught about God in the past.

Revelation is not sealed

Early Unitarianism, as a Protestant church, had a strong sense of the authority of the Bible. Richard Wright advised Unitarian preachers to concentrate on "the plain facts and positive declarations of scripture".[6] However, over the years Unitarianism has come to a more progressive understanding of revelation and authority. Today Unitarians would not accept that one source authoritatively reveals to us the nature and will of God. In other words, "revelation" (what we can and do know religiously) is continuous and progressive.[7] Contemporary Unitarian Andrew Hill expresses it this way: "Our understanding of the Truth is a continuously growing process by which reality slowly discloses its essential nature in response to human effort."[8]

How do we know the Truth? How do we know God? How do we know the will of God? How do we know the nature of God? We don't! That's the starting point. But we are committed to a process of discovery. We are committed to seeking that understanding, seeking revelation, seeking knowledge.

Revelation for the Unitarian is not a once-delivered truth that must now be preached, practised, and defended, but a process of gradually and imperfectly discovering a mysterious truth. Thus Unitarians reject the idea of creeds, as these will fossilise a process that is ever continuing.[9] The truths that have been passed down to us from the past are not dogmas that must be defended, so much as the story-so-far that will be developed. All that we know is provisional (true for now, but we might need to change it in the future) and perspectival (not a "bird's eye view" of the world, but shaped by the particular place we are coming from).[10] This means, as noted by the American Unitarian theologian James Luther Adams, "Nothing is complete, and thus nothing is exempt from criticism".[11]

This can be viewed as an extension of the Protestant suspicion of idolatry.[12] The Truth is a reality beyond our immediate comprehension; therefore it is an act of idolatry for one person or book or institution to be viewed as divinely instituted. That would make such things into God, or God's exclusive representative, and this opens the door to the abuse of power.[13] If I claim to be telling you the certain will of God, then it implies that you should do what I say!

But God cannot be captured in the idol of our ideas, and so we need to be prepared to make radical changes to our ideas if necessary. This has obviously been true of Unitarians historically who rejected one of the most central ideas in Christianity: the Trinity. The fact that it was accepted for centuries as a central truth was not in itself a reason for it to be retained.

So a Unitarian understanding of revelation is best described as "something we have provisionally discovered", rather than "the certain Truth that has been given to us". But how have we discovered it?

Discerning revelation

"Discernment" is a concept with a rich heritage in the Christian tradition. Put simply, discernment is the spiritual practice of making decisions and finding the right path in life. If you are thinking about whether to apply for a job, whether you should move house, whether you should get married, or get divorced, you could be in a place of discernment. The distinction between discernment and simply making a decision may be in the eye of the beholder. But the basic intention is that discernment brings a spiritual dimension to decision making. Discernment is something one might do within the context of prayer, or in the context of a conversation with a spiritual director. It is often described in the language of discerning the will of God in someone's personal life.

But of course there is no certainty in life, as any spiritually mature person would recognise. Life is messy and uncertain, and we feel our way through it as best we can. And so the process of discernment is always one of provisional discovery, rather than following certain and specific instructions from God. This would be recognised by any spiritual director who was offering a listening ear or guidance to someone seeking discernment. Indeed, most spiritual directors might be a little reluctant to encourage a person who said, "I am certain this is God's plan for my life". A more spiritually and emotionally mature person might say, "This *seems* to be the right way forward. I think this is God's plan." There is a natural humility in this attitude.

If this humility is appropriate in the work of personal spirituality, why is it not appropriate in the work of theology? I would suggest that it is. I am suggesting that what is seen as sensible in the realm of personal spiritual discernment should be true of the whole process of theology and mission. We only discern what *seems* to be true, right, good, and beautiful. We are never certain.

I am suggesting that the words of those evangelists on Market Street in Manchester should not be "Here's the truth!" but rather "Here's what seems to us to be true through an imperfect process of trying to work these things out". I am suggesting that Christian missiologists should not be claiming "the mission of God is revealed in the life of Jesus Christ", but rather "the deep experiences of my life (and my community's life) lead me to *experience* the will of God revealed in the life of Jesus Christ".

I am suggesting that, in order to be entirely honest, mission theology has to admit that it might be radically wrong and need to radically change. "Think it possible that you may be mistaken" say the Quakers.[14]

I believe it is worth retaining the concept of the *missio Dei* – the mission of God – but only if it is seen as an expression of what we *don't* know, rather than what we *do*. It should not imply, as it often does in Christian theology, that we have received clear instructions written in stone. Rather it should imply that we really have no idea what we are doing. We are trying to work out the biggest truths of existence. We are struggling with the biggest mystery of all. Of course we are getting it wrong and going down wrong paths. We are trying, and failing, and trying again to discern the mystery of the divine. The complete "will of God" is inherently beyond our understanding. We just don't know what it is. We don't even know if such a phrase is meaningful at all. There is something of the divine that is inherently unknowable. We are lost in a cloud of mystery, cautiously feeling our way through the mist.

But we *do* feel our way through. Some truth, some way forward, *is* possible to discover. How do we do this? How do we discern the truth? How do we discover it, even provisionally? Mainstream Christian theology tends to argue that we discover truth through two different sources: through the "natural" theology that we can derive from the natural world and human experience, and the "revealed" theology that comes from the revelation of the Bible. The Unitarian tradition, however, collapses any distinction between the two.[15] Both are ways of describing the same thing; both are *processes of discovery.*

That discovery is messy and difficult and uncertain. It comes through moments of spiritual insight. It comes through the story of a community. (Mainstream Christianity tends to divide this into "scripture" and "tradition".) It comes through scientific understanding and reason. Nineteenth-century Unitarian theologian James Martineau argued that it came most clearly through conscience, through the inner promptings that tell us the difference between right and wrong.[16] This is the central insight of the Quaker tradition (which in this sense is very close to Martineau's classical Unitarianism), as expressed in the very first sentence of *Advices and Queries,* which reads, "Take heed, dear Friends, to the promptings of love and truth in your hearts. Trust them as the leadings of God whose Light shows us our darkness and brings us to new life."[17]

The central insight of the Quaker tradition is that it is indeed possible for divine revelation to be directly experienced through "the promptings of truth and love in your hearts", experienced within, and discerned and tested by the community. The Unitarian tradition has tended to emphasise much more strongly the insights of reason and science. The theology of Martineau, however, is much closer to the Quaker position, in arguing that the ultimate purpose of Unitarianism is the union of the human and the divine "in the higher region of the soul".[18]

It is through these imperfect processes of heart and mind that we begin to discern revelation, that we begin to get a sense of truth, although it is always partial and never final.

Revelation and tradition

The problem with this process of discerning revelation is that we can make the mistake of interpreting it in a primarily individualistic way. Indeed, this is the mistake that is often made by Unitarians. Following the spirit of the age (and the Enlightenment age when the Unitarian tradition was born), Unitarians often adopt a highly individualistic language and practice of faith.

But we cannot enter into this discernment alone. I do not mean that it is not advisable, I mean that it is literally impossible. The so-called "linguistic turn" in contemporary philosophy has drawn our attention to the fact that all truth and all truth-seeking activities are shaped by linguistic, historical, and social realities of which they are a part. We are not atomised individuals finding a pure truth "for ourselves": we are always one part of a social and historical conversation.

We are always embedded within historical traditions of language and practice.[19] All knowledge and understanding is shaped by our social position and perspective. The revelation that we seem to have discovered is deeply shaped by our particular human experience, and the human experience of those who have gone before us. This means that our faith and theology are shaped by social, political, and economic forces, as has been argued by feminist and liberationist theologians.[20] I am white, male, and British, and so the theology that I am trying to construct here is inevitably shaped by white, male, British experience in ways of which I am not always entirely conscious. There is nothing wrong with this. It is only wrong to be dishonest and claim that it is not the case, with a pretence to some kind of neutrality. I am incapable of seeking truth in a way that is entirely universal and neutral – and so is everybody else.

The claim that revelation is a process of discernment and discovery is not the same thing as saying "the individual should trust his or her own reason and experience, rather than looking to a tradition for answers". The fact is that this is simply impossible. There is no such thing as "naked" reason and experience that has not already been shaped by all kinds of historical traditions.

Let us take the sentence "I am going to trust my own reason and experience, rather than look to tradition for answers". For a start the sentence is written in English. English is itself a tradition that has evolved over hundreds of years. I am capable of writing that sentence only because I have been immersed in the traditions of English all of my life. I am capable of writing that sentence only because I have been supported by an English-speaking community that has shaped me all of my life. It took the input of thousands of people around me to give me the ability to make this statement of individualism.

English is only one language. It expresses things in a certain way. If I had written the sentence in Welsh, it would be subtly different; it would have a slightly different meaning, because one-to-one translation is always impossible, and so translation is always interpretation.

I use the word "reason", which is a concept that has been shaped by three thousand (or more) years of Western philosophy. I may or may not know anything about Socrates or Plato, but the fact is that in my culture my understanding of the definition of "reason" is shaped by such people. I may have heard someone else say "Use your own reason". I may have read the sentence in a book or heard someone say it in a speech. I may or may not remember that, but none of my thoughts is entirely original, and all have been shaped by everything that has happened to me in my life so far.

Other people have taught me how to reason, have taught me what it means. Teachers and parents and everyone with whom I have had a conversation in my life have been part of the school that has taught me how to reason. The fact is that reason and tradition are not in opposition: rather, reasoning is always a practice that has been shaped by a tradition.[21] To "think for yourself" requires a huge societal educational process which gives tools that will allow you to "think for yourself". We can only think for ourselves because we have spent years thinking with others. So our truth-seeking must inevitably be part of a tradition that provides tools, practices, and answers.

This is a challenge to many contemporary Unitarian communities who build publicity on the basis of such individualistic statements. Such statements are philosophically suspect, but also pragmatically self-defeating. Unitarians say, "Come to our community, where you can think for yourself, rather than be bothered by a community that tells you what to think." But if community and tradition are impediments to "thinking for yourself", then would not the best thing be to stay away from all communities? Would it not be better to be alone? To this challenge Unitarians have failed to give a sufficient answer, and therefore a sufficient reason for the existence of Unitarian community.[22] What is the point of community?

One answer to that question in terms of our current exploration is that community is an essential tool for the process of discerning and discovering revelation. Our thinking, feeling, and discerning are tested through a conversation with others in truth-seeking community. And in community we open ourselves to what revelation others have discerned and handed down to us. Revelation is not something once-delivered long ago, but something that lives and flows through the telling and retelling of our stories.

For example, imagine that I go to church and I hear the revelation of the writer of a Hebrew psalm that tells me that God is abounding in steadfast love. I also hear the proclamation of the writer of the First Letter of John, that "God is love". I hear a sermon that explores this topic, and so invites me into a contemporary conversation about love. In hymns and prayers I experience for myself a feeling of love in my heart, my own inner revelation. I also use my own reason to ask, "Could a loving God torture millions in hell?", and my reasoning mind replies, "No, such a thing does not make sense". The revelation of love (and the decision not to believe in hell) is something that I experience both in the present and in the past. I experience it in my own heart, I experience it in the reality of community, and I also experience it by hearing of someone else's revelation from thousands of years ago. It is both an inner spiritual reality and a community story going back generations. And the personal present, the communal present, and the communal past all reinforce one another. They all lead me to the revelation that *God is love.*

That does not mean that I always agree with everything in my tradition and my community. Things are never simple. The philosopher Alasdair MacIntyre defines tradition as "an historically extended, socially embodied argument".[23] But even arguments are *about* something. They have a shared language and subject matter. They are only possible by, in some loose sense at least, belonging to a community.

How do we know what we know? Through an imperfect process of discerning truth in community. Are we certain that it is the full truth of God? We know that it is not, because the mystery is much bigger than our understanding. Is there more to be discovered? Yes there is, and this is a good reason for entering into dialogue with others who hold different truths.

And so we hold to our truth – not just because a community tells us it is true; and not just because we tell ourselves as individuals that it is true; but because we have gone through a communal process, and it *seems* to be true.

What if others discern something different? Well, there is no easy answer to this. It is clear that different groups do hold to different truths. Christian and Muslim evangelists on the same street each give their different messages. In the end it is only possible to say, "This seems true, it feels this way in my gut". This may seem unsatisfactory, but it is at least more honest than Christian theologians who simply assume the truth of their propositions without justifying them. It is more intellectually honest to say, "I don't *know* that this is true, but it feels like this, so this is what I'm going with." And we do have to go with something. We do have to commit to some truth, because we are talking not only about abstract truth here: we are talking about faith, which is about how we live our lives, as much as what we believe. We will explore this further in the next chapter, where I will argue that we do have to live our lives by some kind of faith. We have to choose.

I am aware that the process described in this chapter is a more accurate description of Quakerism than of Unitarianism. In reality, Unitarians have not developed a communal process for discerning questions of truth, and so we largely try to ignore such questions. This is part of the problem in finding a sense of mission, which is why this chapter was necessary. A sense of mission requires having some understanding of truth, and so in this chapter I have tried to show how such questions can be addressed by a liberal community.

To conclude this chapter, let's consider this question: do Unitarians, and other liberal churches, want to grow because they are promoting the Truth? Are they following the will of God in spreading the truth about the one true faith?

The answer has to be no. Liberals, in all honesty, have to make much more humble claims. A liberal theology that is rooted in the mystery of the divine has to say: we have found a bit of the truth, but not all of it. We make no claim to be speaking with the voice of God, or with a God's-eye view of the universe. Indeed, our history shows us that we are often wrong, and we need to update our understandings constantly in the light of new knowledge. But we believe that when we gather into a community we begin to take part in this process of discovery and discernment, which gets us, in a gradual and meandering way, closer to Truth, closer to what might be

God. But our history has also taught us that maybe other people and other communities are on a different meandering path towards the Truth; we cannot guarantee that our path is the one closest to Truth.

This may be a disheartening conclusion. In terms of marketing, simplicity and certainty have a lot going for them. In many ways there is something comforting about someone saying, "Here's the Truth, just come here and believe this". Certainty will always have an appeal to some.

At the same time, some people will equally be put off by certainty. In a spiritual market place it may seem counter-intuitive to be preaching a big "maybe" – but it also displays an honesty that may be refreshing to many people. In post-modern British society it may be a message that speaks to some people more powerfully than a supposed absolute certainty.

But it is not enough by itself. The concept of truth may suggest a series of abstract propositional truths. But that is not really what religion is about. To get to the heart of the matter, we must turn now to the idea of faith. We must turn our attention from "promoting truth" towards "offering salvation".

Questions for reflection and discussion

1. How do you react to the idea of "the mission of God"?

2. Is the message "think for yourself" a self-defeating message for a church? If thinking for yourself is the best thing to do, would it not be better to stay away from any kind of church or community?

3. What are your criteria for deciding whether or not a given idea is true?

4. Given how far Unitarians have gone down the route of individualism, and the resistance to anything that looks like a creed (however provisional), what are the prospects for articulating some shared religious vision?

Endnotes

1 Kirk (1999), p.21.

2 Bosch (1991), pp.389–90.

3 Tillich (1951, p.133) writes: "Christianity claims to be based on the revelation in Jesus as the Christ as the final revelation", but admits that this claim cannot be justified "from anything outside the revelatory situation" (p.133). Compare this with liberal theologian Gordon Kaufman, who writes that "it is impermissible for theologians to take any religious tradition's authoritarian claims about God as an unquestioned foundation for theological work" (Kaufman, 1993, p.28).

4 For example, in the older *Hymns of Worship; Revised* there are 105 hymns beginning with either Father, O Father, God, O God, Lord, or O Lord. In *Hymns for Living* there are only 15 hymns beginning with such a phrase.

5 This phrase was coined by Derek Guiton as what he argued should be the minimum requirement for membership of the Quakers (Guiton, 2015, p.viii).

6 Wright (1824), p.448.

7 This is also related to a this-worldly spirituality, immanent more than transcendent. See Hostler (1981), pp.63–4.

8 Hill (1994), p.10.

9 Hostler writes, "[the view that creeds are unnecessary] carries with it wide implications – far wider indeed than most Unitarians themselves are wont to recognise. To abandon all professions of doctrine as they have done inevitably demands an exceptional willingness to accept changes in belief. The traditional use of a creed is intimately linked with the notion that God has made an initial declaration of his [sic] truth, and that it is the business of the church to preach this revelation and to hand it on unchanged and uncorrupted from one generation to the next... But this historical picture of revelation is wholly inconsistent with the ideal of religious freedom. Rejecting the use of creeds and confessions manifestly implies that God's message to man [sic] is not to be enshrined in such static formulae of belief but ought rather to be expressed in different ways by different people. It requires revelation to be thought of not as a written statement by God but as a spiritual insight by man [sic]; not as a public declaration made once for all, but as a private intuition which each man [sic] can properly understand and express in his [sic] own way in order to extract its full meaning within the context of his [sic] experience and concerns." (Hostler, 1981, pp.24–5.)

10 Saxbee (1994), p.22. See also Wiles (1992), pp.64–5.

11 Adams (1976), p.12.

12 According to Cathal Courtney, writing of belief in the inerrant authority of either scripture or tradition, "both come close to constituting acts of idolatry given that they place a collection of words before the force and power of love which most of them claim they are trying to promote". (Courtney, 2007, p.76.)

13 Adams (1986), p.48. Existentially idolatry is making something penultimate into something ultimate. See Tillich (1951), p.13.

14 Yearly Meeting (1999), 1.02.17.

15 General Assembly of Unitarian and Free Christian Churches (1945), p.70.

16 See Schulman (2002), pp.77–81 and Hall (1950), pp.92–4. See also Hostler (1981), pp.11, 43–4.

17 Yearly Meeting (1999), 1.02.1.

18 Martineau, 1894, quoted in Parke (1985), pp.75–6.

19 Stone writes, "our lives and our practices are always part of a history... or... a tradition. A tradition that is alive and 'in good order' is never a static, finished or once-for-all achievement but is a dynamic process that is responsive to ever-changing historical circumstances" (2007, p.41). For an exploration of the growing realisation that the self is inevitably social, and what this means for liberal theology, see Rasor (2005), p.91. See also Beach (2005), pp.250–1.

20 Cone (1977), pp.41–2.

21 "All reasoning takes place within the context of some traditional mode of thought" (MacIntyre, 1985, p.222).

22 See Millard (2002), pp.122–3 and Hostler (1981), p.76.

23 MacIntyre (1985), p.222.

3 Salvation and the search for faith

Thou who didst come to bring
On thy redeeming wing
Healing and sight,
Health to the sick in mind,
Sight to the inly blind,
Now to all humankind
Let there be light!

"Let There be Light"; words by John Marriott
(Hymn 114 in *Hymns for Living*)

What is salvation?

I recently had a look at the website of a local Evangelical charismatic church. On the front page was a video featuring people who had problems in their lives that were "solved", or at least changed, by "coming to faith" and joining the church. One person had failed to find a spouse when they had seen that as their main purpose in life; another person described taking drugs, getting into fights, and their life being "a total mess"; a third person described having many food allergies that made life difficult. Then each of them said, "But then Jesus changed my life". They each described finding more meaning, becoming more compassionate, and in one example being "healed" of food allergies, because Jesus came into their lives.[1]

What is interesting is that none of them said, "I felt guilty for all I had done wrong, and now I know that I have been forgiven"; or "I was going to hell, but now I know I'm going to heaven". They all described something much more concrete and this-worldly that had changed because they had "accepted Jesus".

This is not unusual. Research seems to suggest that even in mainstream conservative Evangelical churches people who become Christians today in Britain rarely talk in these terms.[2] Quietly and gradually, we have come to a place, at least in British culture, where no one much talks about going to heaven any more.

I give this example simply to demonstrate that "being saved" means something more than "going to heaven", even in conservative Evangelical traditions. We can concentrate entirely on the present life and still talk about "salvation" – but we need to think deeply about what we mean when we use a word like that.

The previous chapter outlined Unitarian understandings of the nature of truth, which present obstacles for any simple understanding of mission as "the promotion of truth". We must now turn to Unitarian understandings of the human condition which present obstacles to any understanding of mission as "the offering of salvation".

Common understandings of a word like "salvation" associate it with an afterlife destination: whether one is going to heaven or to hell. This brings up our first major problem, because historically Unitarians, such as Richard Wright, have been universalist, believing that no one was destined for hell.[3] Unitarians have believed that a good God would not condemn anyone to everlasting hell: we will all be "saved" in the afterlife, and so afterlife "salvation" is not dependent on joining any particular faith tradition.

Today Unitarians are largely agnostic about the afterlife – we just don't know, and we are happy to concentrate on *this* life. But whether a Unitarian view of the afterlife is universalist or agnostic, either way this seems to remove any motivation to evangelise to "save" people from hell. If you don't believe in hell, you can't tell people, "Come to my faith to be saved from hell".

But, as we have seen, the way people actually talk about salvation is as something much more concrete and this-worldly. Even though conservative Evangelical churches may still in theory believe in heaven and hell, in reality what they actually *do* (or at least claim to do) is offer a transformed existence in *this* life. When you ask people about what difference it has made to their life to join a church or "accept Jesus into their hearts", they will talk about love, connection, meaning, healing, but they will very rarely talk about going to heaven.

Does this remove an obstacle that would allow Unitarians to do the same? Can Unitarians offer a transformed existence in this life? Well maybe, but there is another problem, and this *is* a distinct difference between conservatives and liberals, between Evangelicals and Unitarians. Conservative Evangelical Christianity claims that Jesus is the *only* way you can experience a transformed life. So even if we were to interpret "salvation" as something this-worldly, as, broadly, "that which is life-giving in this life", we would still be presented with a problem. The problem is pluralism, an issue that we have already wrestled with, and not entirely solved.

Unitarians, in recognising that revelation is not sealed, are open to the possibility of discerning revelation in other religious traditions. So Unitarians tend towards the opinion that both truth and salvation can come from other religious traditions. A contemporary Unitarian leaflet states that Unitarians "claim no exclusive revelation or status for themselves; and... afford respect and toleration to those who follow different paths of faith".[4] Unitarians "regard the existence of many diverse expressions of faith as inevitable, and also potentially enriching".[5]

Unitarians largely reflect the attitude of broader British culture that lauds pluralism and tolerance and a "live and let live" attitude. Therefore anything that would be seen as "imposing" the Unitarian faith on those of another faith would be seen as unethical, because such an action would be a denial of the validity of the faith of the other. It is in such a culture that words like "mission" and "evangelism" and "salvation" are seen as deeply problematic.

Yet if we accept that Unitarianism does not offer The Truth, can it still offer *a* truth? Even if it is not the only path to salvation, can it still be *a* path to salvation? Even if lots of other paths create human flourishing, can it still offer *a* path to human flourishing?

Before we can begin to answer those questions, we must answer some prior questions. Questions such as: what does it mean to be human? Is there a problem inherent in the human experience? Is there a solution (or more than one solution) to that problem?

Salvation and the human condition

When we speak about human experience, we are seeking to answer a question about the theology of humanity, or theological anthropology. When we ask this question, we come up against a distinctive Unitarian answer which presents yet another obstacle to building a Unitarian theology of salvation and mission.

Unitarianism evolved in opposition to Calvinism ever since the time of Michael Servetus (1511–1553), who personally argued with John Calvin (and came off the worse for it).[6] Richard Wright often defined his mission in opposition to Calvinism. Particularly objectionable to the liberal Unitarian sensibility was the Calvinist view of the depravity of human nature. As such, Unitarianism has always been committed to a positive, optimistic view of human nature.[7]

Unitarians have emphasised humanity's creation in the likeness of God. Contemporary Unitarian Cliff Read has written:

> Unitarians share a positive view of human nature and human potential. While not being blind to human weakness and our capacity for evil, we do not see human beings as inherently depraved or corrupt. We have little time for the doctrines of "original sin" and inherited guilt. Rather we see human beings as having inherent and equal worth ... Unitarians affirm that all human beings originate in the Divine Unity, all have something of God in them, all are alive with the same divine breath.[8]

Nineteenth-century American Unitarian William Ellery Channing wrote, "the Divinity within us ... makes us more and more partakers of the moral perfection of the Supreme Being".[9]

Unfortunately, a wholly positive view of human nature presents an obstacle to our developing an understanding of salvation, as it might suggest that human beings are "just fine as we are, thank you very much". And if humans are just fine, if human existence is just fine, then there can be no theology of salvation, and no substantial mission for a religious community. Even a broad and this-worldly understanding of salvation would be unnecessary.

This is in sharp contrast to any religious community that diagnoses a significant problem in human existence and offers a solution (salvation). Calvinism would claim that humans are sinful, guilty, and in need of forgiveness and salvation to be reconciled with God. That religious view identifies a problem inherent in the human experience and offers a solution. And it does provide an urgent sense of the mission of the church. As we have seen, Evangelical churches are less inclined to talk in this way today, but they will still say very clearly "We see your problems and offer a solution". How can Unitarians do the same if they offer a liberal view that simply says "Human beings are just fine as they are"?

The answer must be that Unitarians have to recognise that human beings are not just fine as they are. A naïvely liberal view of human nature cannot be the last word. That optimistic, wholly positive view of human nature must be seriously qualified, although not entirely rejected. History has simply shown that such a view cannot be maintained.

Unitarianism was a successful religious movement in the nineteenth century, when the doctrines of noble humanity and progress "onwards and upwards forever" seemed to capture the spirit of the times. Just before the First World War the Unitarian van missionaries could optimistically say that "Unitarians have a message of courage and cheer which should be spoken".[10] This attitude was more difficult to maintain in the face of the destructive events of the First World War onwards. Unitarians were, of course, not the only ones reflecting on the human condition in these times. Many Christians began reflecting on this in the twentieth century. The International Missionary Council, meeting in Tambaram, India in 1938, is worth quoting in this naming of the spirit of the time:

> Many have lost all faith. Not only their faith in the gods of
> their fathers; but faith in all they had believed most certain and
> important – in reason and in truth, in honour and in decency, in the
> possibility of peace and the power of right. They are overwhelmed
> by a sense of utter impotence and despair.[11]

It was this spirit that Unitarianism needed to speak to in the twentieth century, but it largely failed to do so. There is an urgent need for a Unitarian anthropology that recognises the ambiguous nature of human nature and the often tragic reality of the human condition.

Unitarians must recognise that the world and human nature do not reflect perfectly the image of the divine. It may be stating the obvious, but it is nevertheless worth saying that we live in a world where things are imperfect: that there *is* a problem in human experience. And it is not merely a technological problem that can be solved by technological thinking. It is not simply that the world is organised in such a way that causes suffering and pain, and if we found the right way to organise it these problems would vanish. That was the thinking of many in the past, and it could be argued that it was the thinking underlying the atrocities of the twentieth century. Technology and technocratic thinking did not lead us to become better human beings, it simply made us more efficient at killing.

Rather, the problem is theological: it is a problem inherent in what it means to be human, and it is a problem that requires a theological solution, or, in other words, salvation.

Salvation and faith

We are now in a position in which we can truly begin to construct our Unitarian mission theology. We have seen the problems inherent in starting from a "top–down", "God's-eye view" theology. We can now begin to start from a "bottom–up" or *existential* starting point. In this context "existential" means relating to the concrete experience of human living, as opposed to an abstract world of ideas. It points us to the feeling, acting, and living of life, rather than just thinking about ideas. So we are not beginning by claiming to know God's plans; rather we are beginning by describing what it means to be human.

Once we recognise that there is a problem or problems in the human condition, we must seek a solution, a theology of salvation (or a soteriology). For there to be a transcending mission for Unitarianism, it must be able to say (if only provisionally) "Here is the problem of human experience, and here is the solution. Here is salvation."

This involves delving into a deeper understanding of salvation. The word is derived from *salvus*, meaning "healthy" or "whole",[12] and so can refer to ultimate existential healing. An existential understanding of salvation would be this-worldly and include such concepts as healing, awakening, flourishing, reconciliation, liberation, and justice.

Some aspects of such an understanding of salvation are more concrete than others. It seems obvious to say that for a starving person salvation is food, and for an oppressed person salvation is liberation. It is tempting for Unitarians to speak only in these terms, but social and political work, as important as they are, cannot be the whole of salvation. Someone may be free and fed, and be diligently working for a world where all are free and fed, but still be suffering from a sense of personal existential meaninglessness. They are still in need of some form of spiritual and existential salvation. And so Unitarian salvation must be existential, it must give hope and meaning in human existence, not merely a political programme for improvement of the world. It must give *faith*.

Why do we need "faith"? For the simple reason that we must live. We must get up in the morning and go about our business with some sense that there is meaning and purpose to life. I am calling this sense of meaning and purpose "faith", and such faith is inescapable for human living. In some broad sense we all must have faith, otherwise we would be spiritually paralysed in life, unable to see any purpose in getting out of bed and getting on with life. All people must have faith, whether that faith is in money, themselves, religion, ambition, hedonism, patriotism, or survival.[13] Nineteenth-century American Unitarian Ralph Waldo Emerson wrote:

> A person will worship something – have no doubt about that. We
> may think our tribute is paid in secret in the dark recesses of our
> hearts – but it will out. That which dominates our imaginations
> and our thoughts will determine our lives, and character. Therefore,
> it behoves us to be careful what we worship, for what we are
> worshipping, we are becoming.[14]

We may try to remain agnostic about "truth" (and perhaps we must), but we cannot remain agnostic about "faith", because to live is to live because of some kind of faith. It is impossible to live without faith. It is impossible not to choose an option.

If you were to try *not* to choose an option, how could you? For example, I can decide that all life is meaningless, but then what do I do with my day? Do I still get up and go to work? If so, why? To make enough money to live on? But this, by definition, shows that I have faith that life is worth living. To make as much money as possible? This demonstrates my faith in wealth. Because I will get in trouble if I don't? This demonstrates my faith that what others think of me is important. The only possibly faithless option is to stay in bed and refuse to eat – and die. Any other action is a faithful one.

In exploring this conception of "faith", I am following the lead of twentieth-century theologian Paul Tillich, who used the term "ultimate concern" to describe faith. I am also following theologian and psychologist James Fowler, himself influenced by Tillich, who wrote:

> Faith is a person's or group's way of moving into the force field of life. It is our way of finding coherence in and giving meaning to the multiple forces and relations that make up our lives. Faith is a person's way of seeing him- or her-self in relation to others against a background of shared meaning and purpose.[15]

Faith is what helps us to deal with the complexities and problems of the human condition. It provides a response to the human problems of suffering, death, injustice, and anxiety. (It may or may not be the *correct* response, but it is *a* response.) It has the power to save us. Tillich wrote:

> Nothing can be of ultimate concern for us if it does not have the power of threatening and saving our being. The term "being"... means the whole of human reality, the structure, the meaning, and the aim of existence. All this is threatened; it can be saved or lost.[16]

This understanding of faith includes traditional "religious" faith, but it is not limited to it. It includes the faith that God loves me and wants something from me, but it also includes the faith that the most important thing is to look after my family, or that I should have as much fun as possible before I die. It may be explicit or implicit. It may be examined or unexamined. It may or may not be the same as the labels that people give themselves (such as "Christian" or "Marxist"), but it is the ultimate set of values and meanings that guide a person's life. If I say "My faith is in the dharma of the Buddha", but this commitment extends to three retreats a year, and the rest of the time what *really* orientates my life is the pursuit of material wealth, then I am ultimately lying (even to myself). In fact my faith is really in the pursuit of wealth – and "the dharma of the Buddha" is a label for a hobby.

For our purposes, although a Unitarian theology will acknowledge the provisional nature of its discoveries, it cannot escape a commitment of faith. Although Unitarian theology can never say with certainty "This is the truth", it *must* say "This is the path". It must present a faith that gives meaning and purpose. If it doesn't, it becomes just a collection of individuals who have faith in themselves, or their understanding of God, or their family, or their reputation, or any number of other kinds of faith, who happen to be connected to the same institution. I would argue that this is to reduce the task of the religious community to a debating society, or social club, or campaigning organisation, or property trustees.

Such a community would inevitably be less appealing than a church that said, "My life was a mess until I met Jesus, and now my life is transformed". More significantly, it is very difficult to say why it would matter whether such a faithless community lived or died. If such a community is not in the business of faith, then it is difficult to see why it matters in the grand scheme of things what happens to it.

Faith, crisis, and conversion

If we do choose a faith, and I have argued that we must do (and already have done), how can we know if our faith is trustworthy and reliable? Is the object of our ultimate trust a worthy one, or one that will prove inadequate in a time of testing? The answer is that it is impossible to know for sure. The liberal commitment to a humble and agnostic position still applies here.

Faith may save us, or it may let us down. In fact, many faiths do prove to be unreliable. If all one's faith rests in a political party, what happens when the election is lost? If all one's faith is in career success, what happens when one is made redundant? If all one's faith is in a charismatic religious leader, what happens when that leader is revealed to be flawed or corrupt? If all one's faith is in a scripture, what happens when one discovers that such scripture is historically flawed?

What happens is a crisis of faith, followed by the seeking and finding of a new faith, in the hope that this one is more reliable. Will this new faith prove to be authentic and trustworthy? Again, there is no way to know for sure. Our commitments must be ultimately provisional, acknowledging the limits of our understanding. But the need for commitment remains inescapable.

The only way to pre-empt a crisis of faith is to hold a faith in a committed but critical manner. Our faith is more likely to be trustworthy if it is an examined faith. If our faith is immune from criticism, then its authenticity can never be tested. But if we enter into a process of the examination of our ultimate concern, our faith, then two outcomes are possible: one is that the faith will survive the testing; the other is that it will not, and a new faith will have to be sought out and found. Either way, the likelihood is that we are closer to finding authentic faith.

Traditional Christian theology argues that there is one trustworthy faith, one truly Ultimate Concern which we may call true religion, true faith, or God. This cannot be spoken of objectively, because we always speak from within a commitment to ultimate concern.[17] As we have explored above, the liberal admits that we can never know this for certain. We can only provisionally commit to faith, knowing that we may be wrong.

The idea of committing "provisionally" should not be confused with committing "half-heartedly". Faith, by its very definition, calls for complete and undivided commitment. Faith is a demand for "conversion", not merely at the moment of crisis and taking on a new faith, but continuously.[18] This sort of conversion (in biblical Greek: *metanoia*) was discussed a great deal by James Luther Adams (1901–1994), the Unitarian Universalist theologian and minister who wrote, "*Metanoia* ... is to be understood as a change of heart, mind, soul – *total* personal orientation".[19] Adams saw the mission of the church as the calling of people to continuous conversion, continuous commitment to faith. An authentic faith tradition asks challenging questions of our faith and ultimate concern. Adams writes: "Religion properly understood is not a sanction for easy inspiration or easy conscience, but rather the source of radical questions regarding our behavior, not only as individuals, but also as members of collectives and corporations."[20] Adams proposed this view of the mission of the liberal church:

> The free church is that community which is committed to
> determining what is rightly of ultimate concern to persons of free
> faith ... When alive, it is the community in which men and women
> are called to seek fulfilment by the surrender of their lives to the
> control of the commanding, sustaining, transforming reality. It is
> the community in which women and men are called to recognise
> and abandon their ever-recurrent reliance on the unreliable. It
> is the community in which the life-spirit of faith tries to create
> and mold life-giving, life-transforming beliefs, the community in
> which persons open themselves to God and to each other and to
> commanding, sustaining, transforming experiences from the past,
> appropriating, criticising and transforming tradition and giving that
> tradition as well as newborn faith the occasion to become relevant
> to the needs of the time.[21]

Such a description enables us to begin to see a Unitarian sense of mission, for such a community is deeply committed to a greater purpose.

Can Unitarians offer salvation? I have argued that they must, that salvation must be this-worldly, and that it must involve the offering of *faith* – a sense of meaning and purpose. The liberal position does not need to say "This is the one true faith" – but it can say "Here is faith that does genuinely offer a deeper way of life". What is that faith? I am aware that I have still not answered this vital question. In dealing with the questions of truth and salvation, we have done no more than cleared the ground and built initial foundations. But these were necessary foundations. At this point it is possible to turn to our main question: what is the purpose of Unitarianism? What self-transcending purpose and message can it offer the world?

Questions for reflection and discussion

1. What connotations did "salvation" have for you before reading this chapter?

2. What is the "existential healing" that you personally long for?

3. Have you experienced a significant change in your life through coming to Unitarianism? Or do you know anyone who has? Reflect on any contemporary Unitarian "salvation stories" that you are aware of.

4. Do you agree that without a shared faith a religious community becomes nothing more than a social club?

Endnotes

1 Liberals may be sceptical of claims of miraculous healing, but the person in question clearly believed they had experienced this healing.

2 See Nash (2014).

3 McLachlan (1998), p.7.

4 Reed, Sampson, and Smith (2007).

5 Reed, Sampson, and Smith (2007).

6 He was burnt at the stake in 1553.

7 Rasor (2005), p.23.

8 Reed (1999), p.21.

9 Rasor (2005), p.26.

10 Roberts (1978), p.188.

11 International Missionary Council (1939), p.15.

12 Tillich (1951), p.146.

13 Beach (2005), pp.291–2.

14 Unitarian Universalist Association (1993), Reading 563.

15 Fowler (1995), p.4.

16 Tillich (1951), p.14.

17 Tillich (1951), p.12.

18 Leach (2003), p.15.

19 Leach (2003), p.9.

20 Leach (2003), p.14 .

21 Leach (2003), p.16.

4 Pluralism or the kindom of God?

Wider grows the kingdom,
Reign of love and light;
For it we must labour,
Till our faith is sight...
Bound by God's far purpose
In one living whole,
Move we on together
To the shining goal!

"Forward Through the Ages"; words by Frederick Lucian Hosmer
(Hymn 208 in *Hymns for Living*)

The real need for faith

As part of my pioneer ministry in Cardiff, I spend a lot of my time among secular activist communities and campaigning organisations. One meeting that I attended was "a space for community to come together to address feelings of isolation and discouragement" prompted by the issue of climate change. This was a group of people who cared deeply about climate change and wanted to do something about it. Some were active in campaigning organisations; others felt that they should be active, but their everyday lives made it difficult to commit themselves. Some people felt guilty that they were not doing more; others felt stuck in a sense of despair. With an issue like climate change, it is very difficult to know where to start, and how to relate one's personal life to the biggest issue that faces humanity in this century.

These were the questions with which that group was wrestling: how can we not lose hope? How can we not burn out and run out of energy? How can we have a community that supports people in this work? How can we

57

not become depressed and despairing? How can we link the personal to the global? How can we not just give the bad news of climate change but give some good news for how the world might be if we took the action that is needed? How do we create the world that we desire in our families, communities, and neighbourhoods, at the same time as in the whole world?

As I have spent time with activists in Cardiff, I have often been in dialogue about these questions. The answer that some activists give is "radical imagination". As Cardiff-based artist and activist Rabab Ghazoul has said, "The radical imagination exists to imagine a future that currently seems out of reach, a future free of racism, war, patriarchy ... we have to imagine it into being in our minds and then pursue this picture in reality, however imaginary".[1]

I would suggest that another name for "radical imagination" could be *faith*. My conclusion from working with activist communities is that what is needed more than anything are faith, hope, community, and a positive vision for what the world could look like. Such a vision would be genuine good news for those trying to change the world.

And this is exactly what faith community (at its best) provides! Faith communities have the potential to offer exactly what is most needed to truly transform the world: hope, community, vision. The question then becomes: does the Unitarian community have the ability to provide such a sense of vision, such good news?

Historically, perhaps, it has struggled to do so. The nineteenth-century Anglican clergyman and theologian F. D. Maurice, who grew up as a Unitarian, wrote

> The question at issue between us is ... not whether [the Unitarians] are good reasoners and I am a bad one, but what Gospel they have to bring to mankind [sic], what light they have to throw on all the questionings and yearnings of the human spirit, what they can show has been done for the deliverance of our race and of its members, what hope they can give us of that which shall yet be done.[2]

This well-informed critic of Unitarianism presents us with a pressing question: what gospel (good news) do Unitarians have to bring to humanity? What hope can Unitarians bring? What faith? We have already explored the problems inherent in asking such a question. We have explored the difficulties of Unitarian mission being seen as "promoting the truth", and I have claimed that Unitarian mission must be much more about provisionally discovering and discerning truth. We have explored the difficulties of Unitarian mission being seen as "offering salvation"; and yet from an existential, this-worldly, perspective I have argued that Unitarianism must present and seek some kind of authentic "saving" faith.

So, what is that faith? What is that "saving" message of faith? What is that vision? It is important to understand what we are *not* talking about here. We are not just talking about an advertising slogan. We are not talking about the kind of poster that some churches put up on their railings, such as, "The blood of Jesus Christ cleanseth us from all sin". It is true that such a message is certainly trying to be a saving message of faith, although one that Unitarians and other liberal Christians reject. But the point is that Unitarians often approach this question as though it is really about what should be put on such posters. British Unitarians have generally approached this question as one of marketing. But we are not in search of an advertising slogan, we are in search of a faith that could be genuinely experienced as good news. We are in search of a whole coherent set of stories, symbols, languages, and practices that, taken together, offer a way of life that diagnoses a problem in human life and offers a solution. We are in search of something that gives coherence and meaning to human life. We are in search of faith. Once we have faith, we can worry about advertising slogans later.

What sort of a faith can Unitarianism offer? It must be one consistent with the Unitarian theology that we have been constructing. It must build on an understanding of the mysterious nature of Truth, which we provisionally discern. It would also have to be a genuine attempt to diagnose the problem of human existence and offer a solution. It would need to avoid a glib response to this challenge. It must, in the words of Paul Tillich, offer a theological answer to an existential question.[3]

It would need to be broadly consistent with the classical Unitarian tradition as it has developed over the centuries. But it must offer a vision of something bigger than self-interest. It must be an attempt to find ultimate concern. This is what many contemporary Unitarian attempts at publicity and promotion fail to do. We point to the church, rather than the faith. The message is generally "We're really good", rather than "Here's a faith that will transform you and the world". In crude terms we could say that the mainstream Christian church says "Jesus is great", the Buddhists say "The dharma of the Buddha is great", Muslims say "Allah is great", but Unitarians say "Unitarians are great". Can you see the difference?

This is why much Unitarian promotion is inherently awkward, and (if I may be frank) a bit embarrassing – because the explicit or implicit message is always "We're great". The only way to avoid this embarrassment is to have a *self-transcending* message, a self-transcending faith, a self-transcending reason for being. There must be a mission that is bigger than the church. There must be a *faith* that is the church's reason for being. There must be a vision that is global, or cosmic.

Faith in pluralism

One possible self-transcending faith could be pluralism itself. Unitarianism is a creedless religious community which refuses to create a creedal test (a particular set of words) for membership or ministry in congregations.[4] A consequence of this approach has been the development of internal theological pluralism. As Unitarians have become more aware of other religions, and as Christian symbols have lost their power for some, individual Unitarians have developed a diversity of religious identities. There may be considerable diversity of beliefs both within and between congregations.

One possible self-transcending purpose for Unitarianism could be the promotion of pluralism. As our communities are so diverse, perhaps we could see the promotion of pluralism as the vision that we offer the world. What the world needs is an acceptance and celebration of diversity. Our vision of the world could be a peaceful one where diversity is celebrated and accepted.

But let's think more deeply about the idea of pluralism. The Unitarian vision of pluralism has often been rooted in an unreflective commitment to an extreme individualism.[5] In this approach Unitarianism has taken on an eclectic and pluralistic approach that is now common to many in our society. The sociologist Stephen Hunt describes contemporary religiosity in this way:

> ... a veritable "spiritual marketplace" has emerged which encourages people to pick and choose until they find a religious identity best suited to their individual, rather than collective, experience – a freedom to seek a religious faith which reflects, endorses, and gives symbolic expression to one's lifestyle and social experience. The contemporary religious environment therefore permits individuals the freedom to discover their own spiritual "truths", their own "reality", and their own "experience" according to what is relevant to their lives.[6]

This is a sociological description of the religious environment of our society for many people. Yet such a vision is often seen as the very essence and purpose of Unitarianism. This claim is of course in itself a theology, a soteriology (a theology of salvation), and an ecclesiology (a theology of the church) and should be reflected upon, although it is often dogmatically and unreflectively accepted by Unitarians.

The most articulate defence of this kind of pluralism is given by Richard Grigg, an American Unitarian Universalist philosopher. Grigg argues that the internal pluralism created by Unitarian Universalism itself offers a symbol of, and reality of, salvation, a faith, a gospel. Grigg argues that pluralism offers an opportunity for what he calls "participation and self-transcendence".[7] He also argues that Unitarian mission in the world should be about modelling and promoting this model of inclusive pluralism in society.[8]

Such a faith in pluralism diagnoses the problem in the human condition as an intolerance towards diversity. The theological solution that it offers is the celebration of diversity and the promotion of pluralism. This does indeed offer a self-transcending vision and purpose for Unitarianism. Its purpose, one much bigger than its own survival, is the promotion of pluralism.

In offering a self-transcending purpose, rooted in a modest understanding that we do not have the whole truth, pluralism does present us with a possible sense of Unitarian mission. It may be a sense of mission that is appealing to many. However, there are a number of serious problems that I would want to highlight.

I would argue that internal Unitarian pluralism is actually something of an illusion. Unitarian congregations do not contain equal numbers of Muslims, Jews, Buddhists, Sikhs, Christians, and atheists. Rather the diversity of Unitarianism is generally across a particular defined spectrum from liberal religious humanist to liberal Christian to a liberal eclecticism embracing all religions. In the (self-selecting) survey that produced the book *Unitarians: Together in Diversity* by Sue Woolley, most correspondents label themselves as some variation of Christian, Pagan, Theist, Humanist, or Universalist.[9] This is not necessarily any more diverse than the Church of England, containing as it does liberals, catholics, and Evangelicals. It is just diverse in a different way. It may even be that in many ways we are *less* theologically diverse than the Church of England: it simply depends on how you calculate theological diversity. Exactly how theological diversity could be calculated (if that is a meaningful question at all) is rarely addressed by advocates of pluralism. But either way it is clear that Unitarians are not as radically diverse as they theoretically could be. Of course, that does not in itself invalidate the argument for pluralism – it could simply evoke the response, "We need to work to become even more diverse". And yet could that diversity contain conservative Christians and conservative Muslims? I don't think it could, and yet such groups represent millions (if not billions) of people in the world. If our pluralism is incapable of containing the largest religious groupings on Earth, then how truly pluralistic is it?

But there are other issues to consider. It is not particularly clear why theological diversity is somehow "better" than diversity of class, age, and race. Again, on that score Unitarians are considerably *less* diverse than other denominations. And this may be indicative of a serious blind-spot. To engage seriously with issues of class and race requires an analysis of power. It requires asking who has the power and wealth, and who does not, and why. The non-white activists whom I know do not talk about "celebrating diversity": they talk about "decolonising". Decolonisation is the process of understanding how white power and imperialism has shaped the world, and how we can overthrow the systems of racism that still shape our society. The language of pluralism, usually promoted by white people, can be an avoidance of the more challenging task of creating an anti-racist and decolonised world.

Equally problematic is that the faith of pluralism is rooted in a Western, post-modern, extreme individualism. It assumes that the most fundamental religious unit is the individual, rather than the community. As such it leaves little justification for community at all. I believe that it cannot offer saving faith because, by definition, it refuses to do so. Although Grigg argues that pluralism itself offers "participation and self-transcendence", it is difficult to see how it can concretely do that. It is difficult to see how pluralism in itself offers meaning, trust, hope, and faith. Cathal Courtney offered a powerful critique of this approach when he wrote that it creates "a meaningless free for all, an anchorless voyage requiring no commitment or dedication, an *à la carte* spirituality that requires nothing from nobody because nothing is very important, a non-conformity for non-conformity's sake, an abdication of the call to search deeply for the meaning of our lives".[10]

Even if it were possible to address these issues, there is still one question that I would put to someone advocating the idea that pluralism is the ultimate mission of Unitarianism: why not just support an interfaith organisation? If our ultimate purpose is to promote pluralism, why not just dissolve all Unitarian communities and funds and donate the money to the Inter Faith Network? If pluralism is the ultimate aim, if our faith is in pluralism above all else, if Unitarianism is really about diversity, then it would surely be a better use of resources to directly promote an interfaith organisation.

That is the logical endpoint of a mission of pluralism. The only other alternative is to stop trying to "include" all other religions under one umbrella and instead embrace an identity as *one* religion among many. I would argue that this is in fact a more meaningful commitment to pluralism. A real and respectful pluralism does not say "Everyone needs to come under our umbrella, which includes all", but rather says "Here we are doing our particular thing – there you are doing your particular thing – and that's OK".

A liberal, pluralistic religious position does not need to say "We're going to be the religion that includes all other religions". It can (and should) say "In this religious community we tell this story, we understand hope and faith this way, but we understand that other communities have a different story and different faith. We can listen and learn from that. We can believe there is truth and salvation in the other stories. But we love *our* story, and it works in our community."

That does not preclude the possibility of a Unitarian, for example, practising Buddhist meditation, or even identifying as a "Buddhist Unitarian". Receiving the rich spiritual gifts of other traditions is still possible. But in such an example, just as the word "Buddhist" refers to a particular set of concrete practices and stories, so similarly the word "Unitarian" should refer to an equally concrete set of practices and stories. When I use the word "Unitarian", I am not referring to a "blank space" in which anything can be slotted, but to a particular historical tradition with its own set of stories and practices.

The Unitarian community needs to embrace its own story, have its own faith and hope that it offers the world. What could that faith look like?

Faith in the kindom of God

I propose that we seek a particular faith by looking into Unitarian history. What faith has existed in the Unitarian tradition? What hope? What sense of purpose beyond mere self-preservation? What sort of language have Unitarians already used? Not very long ago, within living memory, the language that Unitarians used was that of the *kingdom of God*. This can be seen in Unitarian hymns. *Hymns of Worship: Revised*, published in 1962, contained 36 hymns under the sub-title "The Church and the Kingdom of God".[11] The older *Hymns of Worship*, first published in 1927, contained 49 hymns under the section "The Kingdom of God".[12] This is the historic language of Unitarian worship and theology.

This language of faith sits at the very heart and root of the Christian tradition. It is the Greek phrase found in the New Testament, *Basileia tou theou*, the central message of Jesus of Nazareth.[13] Using such a language of faith requires us to see Jesus not as a topic for theology, but as a theologian himself, offering a theological and spiritual vision capable of providing transforming faith. This is consistent with the old Unitarian commitment to the teaching *of* Jesus, rather than the teaching *about* Jesus.

The *Basileia tou theou* is a dominant theme in the Gospels, and most historians would see this idea as the central one preached by Jesus two thousand years ago.[14] But what does it mean? Jesus was frustratingly unclear about this. We only catch glimpses of its meaning in his stories and sayings. But we have some clues. It is a sense of the divine reality breaking through into existence. It is a sense that there is something in the here and now, immanently present. It is never certainly seen or heard, but is fleeting, hidden, just out of sight. It is a whiff of the divine, something within us and around us,[15] something spread across the earth, but not always recognised.[16] It is the smell of the sacred in our nostrils, the feel of the sacred beneath our feet, the glimpse of the sacred on the horizon.

Basileia tou theou is usually translated as "the kingdom of God", but such a phrase is somewhat problematic in the light of feminist critiques of language and the questioning of the appropriateness of "king" as an image for God. Other phrases could be used, such as the Commonwealth, Realm, or Reign of God, and yet none of them is completely satisfactory. One solution is to leave the word untranslated, as we do in the English language with words such as *dharma, Buddha,* and *karma.* I believe this guards against any assumption that we know exactly what the word means, which is important if we are to truly use the phrase appropriately. But such an intellectual Greek phrase does not really work in everyday life, conversations, and worship. From now on I will simply drop the "g" and speak of the *kindom of God.* This has the advantage of suggesting equality, relationship, and kinship, which is one of the themes of the kindom.

What is the kindom of God? The Gospels suggest that it is a saving faith, an ultimate concern. It is something worth selling all you have to buy.[17] You cannot have faith in the kindom of God while simultaneously having faith in wealth:[18] it requires complete loyalty (as all faiths must do). It demands *metanoia*, a complete turning around of values, orientated to ultimate concern, and we are left in no doubt as to the dramatic nature of the conversion. It is a rebirth, a passing from death to life, to awakening, liberation.[19] This is a dramatic process, as any crisis or change of faith must be; but it is worth it.[20] In the words of James Luther Adams, it calls on us to "recognise and abandon [our] ever-recurrent reliance on the unreliable".[21]

The language of the kingdom, or reign, of God suggests that it is a vision of the way God wants the world to be. As such it might seem very similar to the idea of the *missio Dei* – the mission of God. And yet the way in which Jesus uses the phrase suggests, as I already have, that this idea should express what we don't know, as much as what we do. The playful and allusive way in which Jesus speaks about the kindom prevents us from seeing it as a certain plan or agenda for action. Jesus did not say, "Here is the plan of God, it involves this, this, and this". He said, "I want to tell you a story ...". In pondering the stories of Jesus, we are likely to find that the kindom constantly surprises and shocks us. We don't know where we stand. So we only ever provisionally discern the presence of the kindom, we only tentatively discover it here and there. We are never certain.

The kindom of God is mysterious. It cannot be reified or defined. Jesus never gave a direct answer to the question "What is the kindom?" Instead he used metaphors and stories to say what the kindom was *like*.[22] It is like buried treasure, like a seed, like a party. This is not a systematic scheme of truth, but a mysterious reality that we have not fully understood. It demands humility in our understanding of it. Thus Jesus never says that someone has *found* the kindom, only that they are not far from it.[23] Jesus, like many spiritual teachers, remained evasive in playfully pointing to the Divine, but never letting anyone get anywhere near to a clear doctrine or dogma. The Truth remains beyond us.

But that does not mean that it is impossible to discern the presence of the kindom of God. It is discernible in existential, this-worldly terms. Is the kindom present? Well, are the blind seeing? Do the lame walk? Is liberty proclaimed to captives, and good news to the poor?[24] Then the kindom of God is here. It is shown when people and communities live differently: by their fruits you shall know them.[25] This can be seen and judged. It can be discerned.

There is a sense of both present-tense and future-tense dimensions to the kindom of God. It is both the present tense of something happening right now under our noses, and the future tense of the world that we long for, a world of justice and peace. It is both spiritual and political; both the inner transformation of the heart and the goal of justice.[26] It envisages a world where those whose sacred worth has been denied find a place at the table. It is where the outcasts of society[27] and people from the whole world[28] sit down at one abundant banquet. Debts are cancelled.[29] The poorest and most vulnerable are given places of honour.

It operates as an act of "radical imagination" – in imagining the future free of racism, imperialism, war, poverty – while also making this a reality today. It becomes a present-tense reality in each individual soul and also in any faith community that operates by these values. The act of imagining it also creates it.

The faith of the kindom of God is consistent with classical Unitarian theology. It suggests that Truth is beyond our grasp. It naturally fits with a theology and spirituality that is pantheistic or panentheistic, in which the sacred is seen as interconnected with all that is, and as present here and now and not primarily in the past, or the future, or some other realm of existence. It is built on a sense of the sacredness of each human person. It suggests an obligation to work for a more just, loving, and peaceful world. It is ultimately hopeful in affirming the possibility of our achieving such a world within history.

The faith of the kindom of God diagnoses the problem in human life as our alienation from one another and from God. If we examine two of the most central stories told by Jesus, we see this theme. In the story that we label "The Good Samaritan" we see people acting as strangers to the one in need. But the Samaritan acts as a neighbour in having compassion for the one in need on the roadside.[30] We are told to love our neighbour, and told that "neighbour" may mean the stranger who is most different from us.

In the story that we label "The Prodigal Son", a son becomes estranged from his father, and they are, in some sense, dead to one another. But there is an act of reconciliation. There is reconciliation between father and son, although the story ends with uncertainty about whether or not there has been reconciliation between the two brothers.[31]

The faith of the kindom of God offers reconciliation as the self-transcending purpose for a religious community. If the Unitarian community rooted its sense of mission in the kindom of God, it would see its purpose as bringing reconciliation, healing, relationship to a world that is often riven with divisions. But, unlike a faith in pluralism, it does so within a commitment to a particular set of stories provided by Jesus.

The kindom of God in Unitarian and Christian theology

The kindom of God is authentically Christian, it is the teaching of Jesus. I would argue that it is more authentically Christian than churches which claim "The blood of Jesus Christ cleanseth us from all sin" as their message to the world. Theology built on the death of Jesus is theology built by various early Christian writers. But the theology of the kindom of God is the theology of Jesus himself. This is indeed the sort of "primitive" Christianity that was desired by early Unitarians like Richard Wright.

Of course, this could also be seen as a *disadvantage*. Many contemporary Unitarians have a "spiritual allergic reaction" to any Christian language, having come to Unitarianism after bad experiences in some Christian traditions. This provides pastoral and theological challenges in our communities. There is no space here to expound a full argument about the relationship of the Unitarian tradition to the Christian tradition. Perhaps it is honest, though, to acknowledge my general approach to this question. My approach is that classical Unitarianism is both a part of the Christian tradition and also something quite different. Classical Unitarianism fits in a general way within the Christian family of traditions, while also being distinctly different from mainstream Christianity. I have already explored what those differences are in several ways. Nevertheless, sometimes it is a difference of degree rather than kind, and many liberal Christians would agree with the Unitarian approach in many ways. I would hope that many Christians would agree with what I have written about the kindom of God, and I would have no hesitation in trying to persuade any Christian that this idea is at the heart of Christianity.

But it is worth stating how my Unitarian approach to the kindom of God might be different from a mainstream Christian approach. This is not to say that there is not also a lot in common. A number of Christian writers have linked mission to the kindom, and I am indebted to many of them. William Abraham, in *The Logic of Evangelism*, has defined evangelism as "that set of intentional activities which is governed by the goal of initiating people into the kingdom of God for the first time".[32] I am indebted to Abraham for providing this definition, and I have been influenced by this; nevertheless there are some distinct differences.

For William Abraham the kindom of God was started by, and is grounded in, Jesus of Nazareth,[33] in the works of the Holy Spirit at Pentecost, and continually in the community of the kindom – the church.[34] In some sense the kindom of God is the possession of the Christian church. My Unitarian theology does not share this view of the kindom. There is a christological difference here, with Unitarians viewing Jesus as a human who points to something, not as a being who creates a change in reality. I would argue that the authentic words of the historical Jesus do not suggest that the kindom of God is inextricably linked to the person of Jesus, or that it is in any way the possession of the church. Rather, the kindom is something pointed to by Jesus, something that is nearby, at hand,[35] accessible to all, within and among us; it is something spread across the whole earth, but unrecognised by humanity.

The mysterious and indefinable nature of the kindom also enables it to point beyond itself. We never *possess* the kindom: we are always seeking it, and it is always out of reach. This is consistent with the Unitarian view of revelation as something that we seek and discover, rather than something that we have already received fully. It enables us to be open to see the kindom beyond our position, beyond our point of view, beyond our faith commitment, beyond our faith tradition. It may well be that the Christian church is a community of the kindom, but we do not know that it is the *only* community of the kindom. It is a community seeking the kindom.

As I have already stated, in rooting a sense of mission in the symbol of the kindom of God I am making a move that has been made by many other theologians.[36] Such a sense of mission prevents the church from being inward-looking and keeps it looking outwards for the kindom. Theologian Howard Snyder wrote:

Kingdom people seek first the Kingdom of God and its justice;
church people often put church work above concerns of justice,
mercy and truth. Church people think about how to get people into
the church; Kingdom people think about how to get the church into
the world. Church people worry that the world might change the
church; Kingdom people work to see the church change the world.[37]

This may be presenting a somewhat false distinction between kindom and church, but nevertheless it does present a compelling vision of what a kindom-centred faith looks like. This is what it means to have a self-transcending sense of purpose. Not to be primarily concerned with growing the church, but primarily concerned with changing the world. Not to anxiously say "In order to survive we must grow", but to confidently say that we need to recruit for this mission because the world needs us! It means worrying less about getting people into church and worrying more about getting the church into the world.

Faith in Beloved Community

Despite the richness of the symbol of the kindom of God, there may still be some who would question its appropriateness as something that could be the central Unitarian faith. Its ancient biblical language may be powerful in some ways, but alienating in others. If we express the good news in biblical language – "the kindom of God is at hand, turn around and trust in the good news"[38] – it may be meaningless to some and misunderstood by others.

Should the symbol be "translated" into something more meaningful, at least in the context of twenty-first century Western culture? One symbol that could be seen as synonymous with the kindom of God is "the Beloved Community": a phrase perhaps best known from its use by Revd Dr Martin Luther King, Jr.[39] The phrase was created by American philosopher Josiah Royce and developed by theologians at Boston University, where King studied. American church historian Gary Dorrien wrote that for Royce and his followers the Beloved Community "expresses the ethical meaning of the kingdom of God. King taught that the foundation of the beloved community is the divine indwelling that equally graces all people."[40]

Beloved Community is a symbol that can be used for the church itself and for the world community, with peace and justice for all. It is a phrase that sits comfortably in Unitarian language, and some American Unitarian Universalists have passionately argued for it as the centre of faith for Unitarian Universalism.[41] It is a language that points to a sense of mission for American Unitarian Universalism. From my experience of both denominations, I would say that American Unitarian Universalism does have a greater sense of mission than British Unitarianism. This is largely because of a different culture, with a stronger political right wing to battle against. But it is also at least partly because American Unitarian Universalists have built a theological culture around the idea of building Beloved Community in the world.

The American influence on British Unitarianism has meant that it is a phrase that has also been used more and more in a British context. If such a phrase was used, the message could be "We live in a divided and hurting world. Come join a Beloved Community and help to make the world a Beloved Community."

There are many advantages to such a phrase, and yet it has its problems. The term "Beloved Community" does not have as many complex symbolic meanings as the kindom of God. It too easily associates the church itself with the Beloved Community, rather than recognising it as a symbol of the kindom, which refuses to be the sole possession of the church. I believe that "Beloved Community" too easily becomes a gentle argument for a nice church where people get along with each other and have a political programme for improving the world. It loses some of the theological and spiritual power of a symbol which suggests that the sacred is breaking through into life in the here and now.

And so we must ask: does any other language exist to speak about the kindom of God in a way which may make it fresher, and bring deeper theological insights?

Questions for reflection and discussion

1. What is your understanding of the kin(g)dom of God? Do you think it is the same thing as the Beloved Community?

2. "The Unitarian vision of pluralism has often been rooted in an unreflective commitment to an extreme individualism." Does this reflect your personal experience of Unitarianism?

3. Reflect on the diversity (theological and demographic) of your real-world congregation / expression of Unitarianism. Who is not there? Who is present but silent / silenced? Is your Unitarian community more "inward looking" or more "outward looking" to the world (how so)?

Endnotes

1 Personal correspondence.

2 Quoted in Hostler (1981), p.75.

3 Tillich (1951), pp.60–6.

4 This comes from a historical commitment to non-subscription which arises from the theological commitment to the freedom of the individual. This can be traced back in Britain to the Salters' Hall controversy in 1719, when a number of nonconformist ministers refused to subscribe to a statement of belief on principle. See Hostler (1981), pp.20–1.

5 "What a man [sic] is told by his [sic] inmost heart is something that only he [sic] can hear and which may be largely incommunicable to other people: it is for this reason that he [sic] alone can interpret and articulate and no one else can deny his [sic] account of what was said. By making this kind of revelation

the basis of religion Martineau inevitably introduced an attitude of extreme individualism." (Hostler, 1981, p.49.)

6 Hunt (2004), p.35. The similarity of this analysis to Unitarian thought may give cheer that Unitarianism speaks in the same language as religious seekers, but it may also be seen as too similar to contemporary religiosity, so that it does not represent something distinctive that might offer a critique of contemporary religiosity. For an exploration of this tension, see McLaren (2002), pp.155–83.

7 Grigg (2004), p.25.

8 Grigg (2004), pp.94–5.

9 Woolley (2018), pp.14–15.

10 Courtney (2007), p. 47.

11 *Hymns of Worship: Revised*, hymns 211–247.

12 *Hymns of Worship*, hymns 254-295, 613–621.

13 Abraham (1989), p.17.

14 Funk et al. (1993), p.40.

15 Gospel of Luke 17: 20–22; Gospel of Thomas, 3.

16 Gospel of Thomas, 113.

17 Gospel of Matthew 13: 44–46.

18 Gospel of Luke 16: 13.

19 Abraham (1989), pp.82–3.

20 It is a "pearl of great price" (Matthew 13: 45–46).

21 Leach (2003), p.16.

22 Gospel of Luke 13.21; Gospel of Matthew 13: 44.

23 Gospel of Mark 12: 34.

24 Gospel of Matthew 11: 4–6.

25 Gospel of Matthew 7: 16.

26 Knitter (1996), p.117.

27 Gospel of Luke 14: 15–23.

28 Gospel of Luke 13: 29.

29 Gospel of Matthew 6: 12.

30 Gospel of Luke 10: 25–37.

31 Gospel of Luke 15: 11–32.

32 Abraham (1989), p.95.

33 Abraham (1989), p.101.

34 Abraham (1989), p.98.

35 Gospel of Mark 1:15.

36 Knitter (1996), pp.108–11 and Bosch (1991), pp.377–8.

37 Quoted in Bosch (1991), p.378.

38 Gospel of Mark 1:15, paraphrased.

39 King, "Facing the Challenge of a New Age" (1991a), p.140.

40 Quoted in Muir (2016), p.13.

41 See Muir (2016), pp.13–14, and indeed the whole book.

5 Faith in paradise

Show to us again the garden
where all life flows fresh and free.
Gently guide your sons and daughters
into full maturity.
Teach us how to trust each other,
how to use for good our power,
how to touch the earth with reverence.
Then once more will Eden flower.

"Earth Was Given as a Garden"; words by Roberta Bard
(Hymn 32 in *Sing Your Faith*)

The spirituality of paradise

In the autumn of 2016 I was granted a sabbatical from my ministry in Bolton and spent some time travelling through the United States of America. I relied entirely on public transport, flying as little as I could, which was not always easy in the middle of the States. My longest single journey was a fifteen-hour trip on a bus that smelt faintly of vomit, travelling through the night from Chicago to Tulsa, Oklahoma.

My main reason for wanting to stop in Tulsa was to visit All Souls Unitarian Church. The church has a very interesting recent history, as a number of years ago it effectively merged with a black-led Pentecostal church. This happened because the Pentecostal minister, Bishop Carlton Pearson, stopped believing in hell and embraced a theology of universalism, what he called "the gospel of inclusion". For this he was branded a heretic, and most of his huge megachurch left him. But some remained, initially homeless (having lost their building), but eventually finding a home in the Unitarian church, where the last two hundred of them joined.[1]

These Pentecostal, universalist Christians brought their own style of worship with them, and so now All Souls Unitarian Church has a

"Contemporary Service" in addition to other services on a Sunday. It was this Contemporary Service that I visited one beautiful sunny November morning. In the tradition of Evangelical and Pentecostal churches, the worship began with twenty minutes of joyful singing. Then a member of the congregation stood up and welcomed us. With genuine authentic joy this woman said, "You know this morning I got up and I looked at this day, and I thought God must have made it just for me, it was so beautiful." The whole service, which was led entirely by people of colour, radiated a sense of joy and celebration.

It is worth adding that this was two days before America elected a President endorsed by the Ku Klux Klan.[2] There were many good reasons to despair that morning, especially for people of colour in America. But what happened that morning, despite all the despair and darkness in the world, is that we worshipped, we praised, with a genuine sense of joy. The spirituality on display that day is what I would call the spirituality of paradise. In this chapter I want to argue that the spirituality, language, and faith of paradise provide us with a compelling translation of the ideas of Beloved Community and the kindom of God.

This faith in paradise has been explored in the monumental book *Saving Paradise* by Rita Nakashima Brock and Rebecca Ann Parker, which traces *paradise* as a symbol for salvation across two thousand years of Christian theology and art. Parker is recognised as both a United Methodist minister and a Unitarian Universalist minister, and she is the former President of Starr King School for the Ministry (Unitarian Universalist) in Berkeley, California. *Saving Paradise* uncovers the persistent and rich symbol of paradise as a symbol for the church, for salvation, and for the Earth. Brock and Parker argue for this symbol as an authentic alternative to salvation centred on crucifixion and violence. They argue that the symbol of the crucified Christ is found only much later in Christian churches. The earliest Christian churches contain images, not of a dying body on a cross, but of paradise – a natural, earthly scene of peace and beauty.

Paradise is the biblical image of a state of joy and abundance. It is the garden of delights where there is no war, no disconnection, no suffering. However, as Brock and Parker argue, paradise does not just mean a mythical time in the past when all was well. Nor does it refer to a literal place called the Garden of Eden that existed in the past. Nor does it refer only to the afterlife, or to a future when things will be well again. Brock and Parker highlight a Christian spirituality that sees paradise as existing *here and now*, within us and all around us, and within the practices of the Christian church such as the Eucharist and *agape* meals.[3] It is expressed in the hymns of Ephrem the Syrian, a popular Christian hymn writer of the fourth century. These are the kinds of poem and hymn that shaped a great deal of early Christian worship life:

> Paradise surrounds the limbs
> with its many delights;
> the eyes with its handiwork,
> the hearing with its sounds,
> the mouth and the nostrils,
> with its tastes and scents ...
> Paradise raised me up as I perceived it,
> it enriched me as I meditated upon it;
> I forgot my poor estate,
> for it had made me drunk with its fragrance.[4]

I believe that this spirituality of paradise can provide us with a sense of ultimate meaning, can provide us with faith. If paradise is both here and in the future, both in the world and in the worshipping community, then I would argue that it is not too much of an exaggeration to see the word as synonymous with what Jesus meant by the kindom of God. "Paradise" can be another term, like "Beloved Community", that brings a fresh language to the faith of the kindom. The good news of paradise is that the world is beautiful, good, and overflowing with the love and grace of God. But we have to open our eyes to paradise in order to make its full presence realised in the world.

In comparison with the concept of the kindom of God, there are advantages and disadvantages in the concept of paradise. The concept of the kindom is more political and points our attention to the need to transform societal and economic structures. The use of "paradise" could possibly be seen as something softer, gentler, and the language could lose the sharp edge that was no doubt intended by Jesus. Nevertheless, substituting the word "paradise" for "kindom of God" in Jesus' words does produce a striking and fresh effect: "Paradise is like a mustard seed ..."; "paradise is like a man with two sons ..."; "paradise is spread over the whole earth, but people don't see it".

A Unitarian faith based on paradise, much like the kindom of God, and the Beloved Community, would diagnose the problem of human experience as primarily ignorance, somnolence, alienation, and disconnection. Yet the good news is that we already live in paradise. It is within us and all around us. We only need to awaken to its reality and begin to live connected to this felt sense of beauty and love. The message would be "We live in a paradise, but the problem is that we don't see it, and so we abuse it. Open your eyes and see it!"[5] The image of banishment from paradise, alienation from a state of joy and connection to God, to nature, to one another, seems like a resonant existential problem, particularly in our contemporary culture.

Has such a faith been practised by Unitarians? Admittedly such an approach seems at best a minor key in Unitarian history. Perhaps we can detect it in Anna Laetitia Barbauld, who had a vision of worship as something that touched the heart and was not gloomy;[6] but it is shown most fully in the sister tradition of the Universalists, with their deep sense of the love of God, and the belief that "holiness and true happiness are inseparably connected".[7]

The image of paradise also has at least one artistic precedent in British Unitarianism. Golders Green Unitarian Church in north London has as the centre piece of its worship space a vision of paradise in a mural created by the artist Ivon Hitchens RA in 1921. The image is a woodland scene of trees and flowers, with a stream running through it. This idyllic vision is featured in part on the front cover of this book. A pentecostal image of a dove hovers in the top centre. At the top of the mural is the biblical quotation, "The fruit of righteousness is sown in peace" (James 3:18), and at the bottom is the line "The leaves of the trees are for the healing of the nations" (Revelation 22:2). The similarity to paradise art in some early Christian churches is remarkable.[8] This is an image that invites us to see worship itself as entering into paradise.

This faith is also detectable in the work of the American Unitarian poet e. e. cummings. In probably his most famous poem there is a deep sense of joy and awakening in relation to life and the natural world. The first verse reads:

> i thank You God for most this amazing
> day: for the leaping greenly spirits of trees
> and a blue true dream of sky; and for everything
> which is natural which is infinite which is yes ...[9]

– a vision which leads cummings to ask (in the third verse) "how should any human merely being doubt unimaginable You?" What could describe the awakening to paradise better than this?

Ultimately I am making a constructive theological proposal, rather than a historical assertion. I am not arguing that Unitarians have always understood their mission as awakening to paradise, although there is a strong historical precedent for Unitarians seeing their mission as building the kingdom of God or the Beloved Community. I am arguing that the best faith, the best good news that we could articulate at this moment of time, is the good news of paradise.

Love of God

I am not making the claim that this faith and spirituality of paradise belongs exclusively to Unitarians. Indeed, I believe this language of faith points to a spirituality that has been practised by many people, joyful mystics who follow love and let beauty guide them: people like the American poet Walt Whitman (1819–1892), the Persian poet Hafiz (1315–1390), the medieval nun Julian of Norwich, and, of course, Jesus of Nazareth.

But once we turn to mystics such as these, I am aware that we are forced to confront an issue that some might want to avoid. That is the issue of God. Previously I stated that the theology that I was building required an attitude of openness to the possibility of transcendence. Liberal theology must be in some sense agnostic, always open to the possibility of truth beyond our limited understanding. But to remain in a place of uncommitted agnosticism leads ultimately to an uninspiring church and an unsatisfactory faith.

The Genesis story says that God walked freely with humans in the Garden of Eden "at the time of the evening breeze",[10] and so the spirituality and theology of paradise is incomplete if it does not include intimate friendship with God. Indeed, a love relationship with God is the very foundation of the theology that I am attempting to build here. At this point in our theological journey I am advocating not just an openness to the possibility of transcendence, but an openness to the possibility of relationship with a personal God.

I am aware that this could be the most controversial part of my entire argument. Unitarians, Quakers, and even some progressive Christians have tended to speak of the divine in highly impersonal and abstract terms, as "that which they believe to be of supreme worth".[11] Some deny the worth of the word entirely and embrace atheism and humanism. In such an environment it feels like the taboo of all taboos to build a Unitarian sense of mission rooted in the love of God. And yet this is at the heart of classical Unitarianism, certainly the Unitarianism practised by Richard Wright. Not too long ago the widely acknowledged "first principle" of Unitarianism was "the Fatherhood of God".[12] When speaking about this today, the conversation has generally been around gender. Today, we would not want to speak about the fatherhood of God without also speaking about the motherhood of God. I fully endorse this. And yet the bigger point is that God has the character of a loving parent. It is possible to embrace feminist theology (as I do) while still holding to this central insight – God loves us. I don't expect to be able to persuade those who are convinced humanists, but I do want to make a stand for a theology rooted in classical Unitarianism. For those who are still open to the possibility of the love of God, this faith is still a viable, living possibility.

Some may object that this personal language of God seems a bit infantile, something a bit beneath sophisticated liberals. The trend in recent decades has been more towards a language of energy, power, light, and love. There is much that such language can bring to us, and yet sometimes such language keeps us in the shallow end of spirituality. Derek Guiton, in his book *A Man that Looks on Glass: Standing up for God in the Religious Society of Friends (Quakers)*, makes an impassioned argument for God (a personal God) in the Quaker context. He quotes fellow Quaker Rachel Britton in arguing that "person" is "the richest metaphor we have for God, because only the person is conscious, is self-aware, only the person can know and love persons, can discern truth or have purposes".[13]

Today it is often the liberal instinct to speak in impersonal terms of Love and Light. But how can it be meaningful to speak of Love without a Lover? Only a "person" (in some sense) has the ability to love. A force or energy cannot love. A religion rooted in the spiritual experience of Love only really makes sense if there is some kind of a loving "person" who is capable of saying, "You are my Beloved, with you I am well pleased".

On paper, the Unitarian denomination still has as one of its prime purposes "the worship of God",[14] and yet in practice perhaps the idea of worship of and prayer to God seems to have dropped away. As Art Lester preached at the Unitarian Anniversary Service in 2008:

> It may be that we have stopped viewing God as someone you can really talk to. If that is so, then the happy-clappies have it all over us. Maybe God and the Spirit and all that have become nothing more than an idea, a topic for discussion. Maybe it means that we think that God isn't really there at all, that He has joined the mobs in the great drive-in temples of loony America, and left us to merely philosophise. And if God doesn't make an appearance in church on Sunday, how can we expect to see anyone who is actually looking for Him?
>
> Our failing is not one of hypnotising the throngs with guitar chords and rhetoric as the evangelicals do; it is that we often attempt to worship an idea. You can't worship an idea. You can't fall to your knees before an opinion, and you can't find yourself weeping with pity and love over a finely-turned philosophical argument. The question of why we are declining may have an answer that is at once simple and complex. Simple because it can be expressed in a single sentence. Complex because it may entail some re-thinking of our customs, our activities and – yes – even our theology. I think I might put it in another question: *are we nourishing the soul?*[15]

The argument that we should expect God to "make an appearance in church on Sunday" – indeed that *inviting* that appearance is primarily what worship is – will be controversial in a post-modern, pluralistic Unitarian context. But part of the point is that personal experience, not argument, is what it is all about. The point is that a personal relationship with God must be personally experienced. The writing of the mystics can witness to a living relationship with God, but only serve to point us to finding that relationship ourselves. Ultimately it is only in prayer and worship that a real relationship with the Living God can be discovered. A community with faith in paradise is a worshipping community where people are invited into communal and personal spiritual practices that enable each person to experience God for themselves. I freely admit that my thinking in this is shaped by the Quaker tradition, with its central insight that each person is capable of being a mystic and directly experiencing God. "Take heed, dear Friends, to the promptings of love and truth in your hearts. Trust them as the leadings of God whose Light shows us our darkness and brings us to new life."[16]

In a liberal faith the dependability of a personal relationship with God must always be balanced with the doubt of agnosticism. Without that doubt, it is too easy to descend into superstition or fanaticism. To know God is not to know everything about God. To experience God is not to receive certain instruction from God. A real mystical faith experiences both the light of knowing and the darkness of unknowing. But just as thinking that one knows the mind of God can lead to fanaticism, so equally thinking that God is too abstract or impersonal to be known can lead to an uncommitted and weak, wishy-washy liberalism.

I have already argued that we know what we know religiously through discernment: through a personal and communal process of listening to the stories of others, and opening to religious experience. This is an imperfect process which does not produce clear-cut answers. And yet if there is one thing I know, as certainly as I can know anything, it is that God is love. That is the conclusion of many communities and individuals, and it is my conclusion. It seems only honest to admit that this is the centre of my personal theology, and the commitment out of which all else flows.

I have been attempting to construct a theology of mission based on paradise. But even this language may be too abstract, requiring too much explanation in an everyday conversational context. In such a context it is worth considering the simple articulation of "good news" as being simply "God loves you". I would ask whether anything Unitarians have written as publicity for the last fifty years comes anywhere near the simplicity, power, and effectiveness of this message.

And it is effective. Is it too simplistic to say that churches that invite people into a personal relationship with God are growing, and those that don't are declining? I cannot claim to have done the research to prove this, but I would suggest that it *may* be true, and if so it is a staggeringly simple and challenging conclusion that liberals should consider.[17]

The most practical difference that this makes is in our approach to worship. A theology of paradise invites us to see worship as primarily about experiencing the presence of the Living God, as opposed to a chance for some intellectual stimulation. Unitarianism's sermon-centred worship has historically tended to be the latter, as has much of the Protestant nonconformist tradition. Services have been a chance to think – to be mentally stimulated. But I would concur with Art Lester's challenge here in insisting that this *does not* nourish the soul. What nourishes the soul is worship that is primarily based on prayer and praise (in whatever outward form that comes).

One other theological issue is worth considering here – and that is grace. Grace is the theological concept that says that the salvation we receive is a gift given, not a reward earned. This is a concept more central to historic American Universalism than to British Unitarianism. Rebecca Parker writes that Universalism was rooted in "a deep religious intuition that all of our lives are unquestionably grounded in grace".[18] But there is a tension, even a contradiction, here with the more Unitarian and liberal Protestant approach, and it is a tension directly relevant to our task here.

The question is: do *we* build paradise, or does God? In building this theology of mission, am I saying that *our* mission is to build paradise on Earth with our own sweat and tears, or to simply observe that God is already doing so? Historically Unitarians, along with other liberal Christians, believed that it was *our* job to do it. Again, Rebecca Parker writes that she was "shaped by the tradition of liberal, social gospel Christianity. I was raised believing ... that the Kingdom of God will be realised on earth

... but we have to build it".[19] This is the theology that underpins liberal commitments to social justice and prophetic witness. Many would argue that this is an essential component of religious liberalism, and something to be proud of.

But what happens when things go wrong? As Rebecca Parker writes,

> We despair. On a personal level, many of us come to a life crisis that forces us to face the fact that there is something broken in this world – in ourselves, our families, our churches, our workplaces, our communities – that for all our ingenuity, commitment, and genius we cannot fix. We come up against helplessness, the inability to stop loved ones from dying, or turn our children from paths of self-destruction, or keep riots from happening. Sometimes we can't even get our own churches to be places where people are civil to one another. We come up against the limits of our faith. We may find ourselves asking, "Is there any source of help beyond my own strength?"[20]

Without a sense of transcendent grace, there is no answer to such a question. We have to just keep plodding on in our own strength, even when we feel utterly full of despair and hopelessness. This, I would suggest, is the shadow of the American Unitarian Universalist commitment to building Beloved Community through social-justice work. I believe that in these comments Parker is identifying a culture of anxiety and despair that is always below the surface for a community with a strong sense of responsibility to change the world.

But with a sense of grace, a sense of the love of God, a faith in something bigger than us, we can find sources of hope and strength that enable us to keep going. Mission rooted in paradise embraces the paradox: we do have to work to create paradise on Earth ourselves, while also with a sense that we are only discovering what God has already done. Paradise is now – and also not yet. It is entirely our responsibility – and entirely God's. We must make paradise, but in fact we are only seeking the paradise that already exists. This seems like a contradiction, but it creates the attitude, the faith, the hope that we truly need.

It may be possible to go along with my theology of paradise, while having reservations about the language and spirituality of a personal God. I expect that this will be the view of many readers. But doing so may cut us off from a theological language, and spiritual experience, that is both the most simple and also the most profound.

Love of neighbour

The faith of paradise points us not only inwards, towards God, but also outwards towards the world. Ultimately this is one and the same thing. The word *Unitarian* points us towards a spiritual insight taught by many mystics – that is *the oneness of everything*. Twentieth-century Catholic monk Thomas Merton described an experience that gives an insight that is typical of many mystics:

> In Louisville, at the corner of Fourth and Walnut, in the center of the shopping district, I was suddenly overwhelmed with the realization that I loved all those people, that they were mine and I theirs, that we could not be alien to one another even though we were total strangers. It was like waking from a dream of separateness, of spurious self-isolation in a special world, the world of renunciation and supposed holiness. The whole illusion of a separate holy existence is a dream...
>
> This sense of liberation from an illusory difference was such a relief and such a joy to me that I almost laughed out loud...
>
> There is no way of telling people that they are all walking around shining like the sun.
>
> There are no strangers!
>
> If only we could see each other [as we really are] ... all the time. There would be no more war, no more hatred, no more cruelty, no more greed ... I suppose the big problem would be that we would fall down and worship each other...
>
> The gate of heaven is everywhere.[21]

If "the gate of heaven is everywhere", then our spiritual task becomes not just to love God, but also to love the Earth. This is the strongest argument for a paradise spirituality in the twenty-first century.

We are currently living through a global climate crisis caused by human activity. Carbon released into the atmosphere by human industry and agriculture is radically shifting the climate towards a warmer and more volatile planet. This is already affecting millions of people, largely in equatorial regions, with increased floods and droughts. If humanity does not limit the warming of the Earth to below 1.5 degrees Celsius above pre-industrial levels, then we will be in unprecedentedly dangerous territory. In this context a faith based on paradise calls upon us to love the Earth and non-human nature. Our sense of "neighbour" must include both humans around the world already suffering the effects of climate change and also animals and plants in need of saving.

Many people are deeply concerned about the state of the world and want to do something about it. And yet the obstacles against effective action are huge. It will take a revolution of our political and economic order. The cause is (almost) hopeless. Effective action against climate change will take acts of "radical imagination" that provide a vision of the beauty of the world that we have to save. Paradise provides such a vision of the radical imagination.

Paradise is about a relationship with the world. This involves us humans not seeing ourselves as above and beyond nature, but as siblings in creation, members of the same family. We must embrace our own animal natures. The spirituality of which we are capable makes humans, perhaps, unique in the animal world, but it should not alienate us from our own bodily animal natures. Too much Western religion has done this – has made spirituality operate in opposition to the body. But Adam and Eve in the Eden story were "naked and not ashamed".[22] Our spiritual task is to return to this paradise state. In a society where so many feel shame about their own bodies (and their sense of self), there is an urgent need for us to get back to right relationship both with the Earth and with our bodies that are part of the Earth. The spirituality of paradise invites us to a deeper sensuality that delights in the body and the senses. In the words of Ephrem the Syrian:

Let us see those things that He does for us every day!
How many tastes for the mouth! How many beauties for the eye!
How many melodies for the ear! How many scents for the nostrils!
Who is sufficient in comparison to the goodness of these little things?[23]

Such a sensuality builds a theology that has a positive relationship to the body, the senses, and sexuality. It is not about denying the delights of physical existence as "unspiritual", but about seeing them as deeply imbued with divinity. Loving our neighbour involves loving self, including the body.

I am aware that there may be objections to the faith and spirituality that I am advocating. The danger of this poetic, nature-loving, joyful spirituality is that it can seem too optimistic, and not treat pain, suffering, and injustice with enough seriousness. As I observed in Chapter 3, liberal theology has often been too weak in naming and acknowledging the suffering of the world. This is a serious criticism, and it must be addressed. Perhaps to truly love our neighbour, to create justice in this world, we must acknowledge that the world is a place of pain and suffering.

In the face of genocide, climate change, and personal suffering, is it appropriate to promote the message that "we live in paradise"? This may sound comically, even bitterly, ironic. For those suffering under injustices of poverty, exploitation, or racism, it may seem insulting. Would the people suffering under poverty in the slums in Liverpool in the 1830s have responded if this was the message of the domestic missionaries?

Paradise points to a deep sense of beauty and love in this world, but this is not the same thing as saying, "The world is just lovely and fine as it is". Indeed there are forces of death and destruction that constantly attack paradise. Our alienation from paradise has created whole economic and political systems that perpetuate *more* alienation. These systems create poverty for many, and dissatisfaction for all. We are tricked into seeking to overcome our alienation by working harder, earning more, and buying more. But this perpetuates the system that continues to destroy the environment and create more problems.

Just as Jesus' kingdom of God suggests a contrast with the kingdom of Caesar, so the faith of paradise has its opposite in the life-destroying system of the world. This system has been named in different ways as "The Domination System" or "The Powers that Be".[24] It is the system of violence, militarism, and economic exploitation that creates and perpetuates poverty, alienation, and environmental destruction. The point is that these evils in our world are not just the result of lots of individuals making bad decisions. They are the result of *a faith* that demands as much loyalty and worship as any other faith. Advertising, political culture, and economic systems constantly preach to us that this Domination System is what deserves our service, allegiance, and faith. Radical imagination is what enables us to imagine *a different world*, but the Domination System fights for control of our imaginations, to make sure that we have faith in its system and *can't* imagine any other world.

The Domination System has been named in different ways, but the activists of my acquaintance usually name it as Empire.[25] *Empire* refers to a whole system of racial, economic, and ecological exploitation. It includes the British Empire but also includes the empires of high capitalism that still exist in the twenty-first century. Many activists see the context of all of their work as the work of decolonising. This is nothing new. We should not forget that the context of Jesus and his ministry was an occupied nation under the domination of the Roman Empire.

And so our question becomes: does faith in paradise have the ability to challenge Empire? Can a spirituality of paradise shape people who are resistant to exploitation or serious suffering? There is an argument for it. It was the teaching of the early Christian church that human beings could resist evil only by becoming deeply attuned to the divine presence within and all around.[26] Ephrem the Syrian wrote his ecstatic hymns of paradise from a fourth-century war zone.[27] Perhaps the only way to be an activist is first to be a mystic.

Is that realistic? Is it possible to confront the evils of the world with paradise in your eyes? It is certainly not easy, and I would not be personally convinced myself if I had not seen evidence of it from people resisting extreme evil. Etty Hillesum provides such evidence. She was a Dutch Jew suffering under the Nazi occupation in Amsterdam. She was later deported to Poland and murdered, like millions of other Jews, in a concentration camp. Her diary and letters were subsequently discovered and published.

They present a formidable intellectual and spiritual mind. She lived a joyful and love-full spirituality that is demonstrated by a letter that she wrote in August 1943, just three months before she was killed. It began:

> This morning there was a rainbow over the camp, and the sun shone in the mud puddles. When I went into the hospital barracks, some of the women called out, "Have you got good news? You look so cheerful." I considered saying something ... about peace being on the way. I couldn't fob them off with the rainbow, could I? – even though that was the only reason for my cheerfulness.[28]

I am not suggesting that Etty Hillesum was constantly "cheerful" in a concentration camp in the sense of cultivating a silly attitude of denial. She was well aware of the horror of her situation. What I am suggesting is that a faith rooted in a deep sense of beauty and love and grace in this world can give joy and meaning, even in the face of the greatest horror, can provide the imagination with a sense of hope, a sense that another world is possible, is here, and is more real than the world of violence and Empire. That is what it means to see paradise in this world.

This is not an argument for a personal attitude of cheerfulness. I am not arguing for "being in a good mood" all the time. Naturally in life, not just in extreme circumstances but in the ordinariness of life, there are times when we are happier, and times when we are grumpier. Paradise is a *faith*, not a mood. That means that, independent of personal circumstances or particular mood, there is a deeper sense of hope. It is true that suffering does offer a challenge to the faith in paradise, and I do not want to glibly ignore or downplay suffering. There is a danger of being naïve here, but I am provisionally hopeful that faith in paradise is not destroyed by the reality of suffering.

Faith lives in the irony and the paradox. Paradise is both present tense and future tense. It is the future that we are seeking, where forces of evil and Empire will be defeated. Yet we defeat those evils by living the values of paradise right now.

In the twenty-first century a sense of paradise may well be the most fruitful faith for Unitarians to preach and practise. As an interpretation of Jesus' teaching of the kindom of God, it invites love of God, neighbour, self, and Earth. But I am happy to admit that theology is often about playing with different languages. And so if people prefer to use the terms "kindom of God" or "Beloved Community", I am quite comfortable with that. These terms are ultimately interchangeable; and there may be others that I have not considered which could be equally fruitful.

But whether "paradise", "kindom of God", or "Beloved Community" is used, the function is the same. These terms are visions of the radical imagination. They imagine a possible future and create the future through the act of imagining. They point to a faith in "the commanding, sustaining, transforming reality"[29] that exists in the present tense, while also inviting us into a better future. They can provide a self-transcending sense of purpose for a liberal church. They could provide Unitarians with a mission bigger than mere self-preservation.

Paradise and community

My task here, attempting to articulate a self-transcending faith and mission in a Unitarian context, is of course theoretical. This may all sound very nice in theory, but I must emphasise that it is a pointless task unless there is a way in which these ideas can be given concrete expression in the lives of individuals and communities.

The greatest barrier to this happening, in the words of American Unitarian Universalist minister Fredric Muir, is "a persistent, pervasive, disturbing, and disruptive commitment to individualism that misguides our ability to engage the changing times".[30] It is this commitment to individualism that is the greatest barrier to Unitarianism living out the call of paradise as a self-transcending mission.

This commitment to individualism has led to a weak sense of community, and it is only in strong community that the values of paradise can truly be lived out. There is always a balance that needs to be struck between the two poles of community and individual. When the community is dominant over the individual, dissent and diversity can be crushed in the name of the greater good. This can be oppressive and damaging to individuals. Liberals have always been wary of this danger. But there are also dangers in the balance shifting in the other direction – when the needs of the individual always dominate the needs of the community. This can lead to dysfunctional, uncommitted, self-indulgent communities that have no sense of mission. Unitarians have been far too unbalanced towards individualism for too long, and I would argue, along with Fredric Muir, that "shifting demographics, economic realities, and concerns on the global stage require more and more *interdependence*, [therefore] we need to re-story what it means to be an individual in community, what it means to be Unitarian".[31]

Fortunately there are resources in Unitarian history for this "re-storying" from individualism to interdependence. Instead of beginning our story with the rationalistic liberalism of the eighteenth-century British Enlightenment, perhaps we need to start further back. In the sixteenth century in Poland there was a Unitarian movement (now extinct) that was rooted in the radical Anabaptist tradition. In very broad brushstrokes we could portray Enlightenment liberalism as scientific, individualistic, and capitalistic. But Anabaptist radicalism was biblical, communitarian, and socialist. Enlightenment liberalism was about freedom, and the individual. Anabaptist radicalism was about commitment and community.

I would maintain that one without the other is lopsided and likely to get into trouble. In contemporary times the Enlightenment liberalism is dominant, but in the future I believe we will need to turn much more to Anabaptist radicalism. The Polish Unitarian community required considerable commitment of its members. Members rejected violence and embraced pacifism, and some wealthy members gave away nearly all of their riches to the poor.[32]

Faith in paradise requires such radical, counter-cultural values if it is to challenge Empire. If it is truly rooted in the teaching of Jesus, it requires communities living by values of simplicity, humility, compassion, hospitality, justice, equality, love, and non-violence. Bryan Stone, a Methodist theologian of evangelism, advocates these values as underpinning mission in his book *Evangelism After Christendom*. He argues that mission is not a matter of presenting clever slogans or slick advertising. It is not a matter of getting "the message" right. It is rather about witnessing to the church's values and stories in everything that it does, and the way that it does it. It is demonstrating in the lives of individual Christians and the life of the church a commitment to the kindom of God expressed in a coherent set of stories, practices, and virtues that enable resistance to Empire. It is demonstrating in the church a "distinctive set of habits, practices, disciplines and loyalties that together constitute a visible and recognizable pattern before a watching world".[33]

There are particular Irish and British antecedents for this view of the nature of church. Early Anglo-Saxon and Celtic monastic communities viewed their purpose in the world as being outposts of paradise. Writing about sixth-century Irish missionary monk Columbanus, Philip Sheldrake observes:

> Monks in the tradition of Columbanus saw monastic settlements as anticipations of paradise in which the forces of division, violence and evil were excluded. Wild beasts were tamed and nature was regulated. The privileges of Adam and Eve in Eden, received from God but lost in the Fall, were reclaimed. The living out of this vision of an alternative world involved all the people who were brought within the enclosed space. It was not something that concerned merely the "professional" ascetics. The Columbanian tradition, for example, believed that all people were called from birth to the experience of contemplation. So, "monastic" enclosures were places of spiritual experience and non-violence and also places of education, wisdom and art. Within the enclosures there took place, ideally speaking, an integration of all the elements of human life, as well as of all classes of human society.[34]

This history provides a model for Unitarian community that is a visible and recognisable pattern of paradise in today's world. This is what a community looks like when it is seeking paradise by living as an outpost of paradise. What does this mean? It means that humans will live in a relationship of equality, including equality between men and women. ("When Adam delved, and Eve span, who was then the gentleman?" asked the radical English priest John Ball before the Peasants' Revolt in 1381.) It will be a community living in right relationship with animals and plants and the earth. It will be a Beloved Community of joy and celebration where all feast together at one table (ideally, literally). It will be a community where God is known walking on earth, not hidden away in the skies. It will be a community that rejects violence and wealth and Empire and all that separates us from paradise.

If paradise is to become more than a clever idea, it will have to be embodied in communities living by such values and habits. Such communities will try to operate as outposts of paradise, often living counter-cultural values. They will invite others to "come and see" what paradise looks like, and offer concrete spiritual practices that will invite all into the presence of God. They will also demonstrate that the spiritual path requires commitment and discipline. They will not say "Come here and we will support your individual spiritual journey", but will say, "Here is the spiritual discipline that this community offers. It is not easy, but it is a genuine path of transformation." Such communities will see their mission as inviting people to a transformation of their spiritual, personal, political, and economic lives, not just a change in their beliefs, affiliation, or church attendance.

The danger here, of course, is that I am being hopelessly and unrealistically idealistic. Of course, in real life community is hard work, and real people are frustratingly difficult to deal with! I am not suggesting that a community of paradise will have no conflict or difficulties. But I am suggesting that we can and we should have higher expectations for how community can be, even when such expectations will inevitably be tested through hard times.

So do such communities that I have been describing already exist? Or is this just a pipe dream? I do see hints of such communities existing here and there: enough to keep me hopeful that paradise is possible. All Souls in Tulsa shows how some of these values are being lived out on the scale of a very large church. Another example is Original Blessing, a Unitarian Universalist community in New York City which defines its mission as helping people to "experience God" so that we can "restore a sacred relationship with our planet".[35] But I suspect that most of the communities embodying these values are small (perhaps tiny) and operating "under the radar". Many of them might not even seem to be "churches". For example, the Lucy Stone Cooperative is an eleven-bedroom house in Boston where residents commit to living by certain values and gather every Sunday night for a shared meal and worship.[36]

In a British context I am not aware of such communities existing that are affiliated to Unitarianism. But there are a lot of communities operating in our culture that are experimenting with new ways of being church. I have friends who are devoted to justice and faith but who feel quite ambivalent about institutional churches. They are deeply committed to a weekly house meeting with prayer, food, and support, but they are not necessarily in "church" on a Sunday morning.

In my work in Cardiff I do see glimpses of paradise. I see seeds of what I am talking about here in people who are seeking to integrate spirituality and activism. I see people committed to community, to the inner work and the outer work, to a spirituality that resists Empire. Seeds of paradise are scattered everywhere, and I remain hopeful for growth.

It is only at this point in our journey that we can return to the question of church growth. It is perfectly legitimate to seek the numerical growth of the church if we believe that the church is an instrument of paradise. The church is not an end in itself. It is only ever a means to an end, although an important one. The end, the mission of the church, is seeking paradise. The mission is about individuals and the world growing closer to paradise and resisting Empire. We invite people to find and create paradise with us, and be initiated into the habits of paradise. However, it is not for the sake of itself, it is always for the sake of the world. The growth agenda must be subsumed within the paradise agenda. If the two are in conflict, then the paradise agenda should always come first.[37]

We have finally arrived at the answer to the "why?" question. Why should we desire the growth of our liberal denomination? Because the world is suffering from alienation and injustice and Empire. People are alienated from the Earth, from their own bodies, from their neighbours, and from God (the insights of mystics suggest that these are all the same thing). In such a world we must grow to offer a vision of paradise, a vision of the radical imagination that introduces people to the reality of their oneness with all and a vision of how the world could be. We must show how this is possible by being an outpost of paradise, by concretely demonstrating how paradise can be a reality in this world and in our congregations. We must replace the world's imagination of Empire with an imagination of paradise. We want to recruit people to this mission because of the great needs of the world.

What is our message? Our good news? That you live in paradise, and that the powers of Empire have lied to you. In some circumstances, if we are bold enough, perhaps the message could even be that God loves you; that the fundamental reality of the world is relationship, and not isolation – but we each have to discover this for ourselves.

This is my best attempt at liberal good news, my best attempt at providing a Unitarian reason for growth. But the task is not over yet. Now that we have a theological foundation, we must turn our attention to more concrete and practical problems. Now that we have answered the "why" question of mission, we must attempt an answer to the "how" question of mission.

Questions for reflection and discussion

1. Kin(g)dom / Beloved Community / Paradise. Which of these metaphors most speaks to you in your despair? Which stirs you to act for justice?

2. What do you understand by a "loving relationship with a personal God"?

3. In your experience, what is the heart of the Unitarian worship experience: preaching? Prayer? Something else? How does this shape our vision?

4. In the face of suffering, is the message of paradise too hopeful, too positive?

5. How could you imagine your congregation (or an alternative expression of Unitarianism) acting as a visible "outpost of paradise"?

6. Can you identify some "seeds of paradise" that you have personally witnessed in the world (i.e. in your local community – not necessarily in church)?

Endnotes

1   French (2009).

2   Hooton (2016).

3   Brock and Parker (2012), pp.55, 141–68.

4   Brock and Parker (2012), p.95.

5   This might be a different way of saying what was claimed in the Unitarian report *A Free Religious Faith*: that the universe is rational, moral, and beautiful, and that the universe is a spiritual reality (General Assembly of Unitarian and Free Christian Churches (1945), pp.13–18).

6   Barbauld (2000), p.479.

7   "Winchester Profession" (1803) , quoted in Cassara (1997), p.110.

8   See, for example, Brock and Parker (2012), pp.86–8.

9   *Xaipe* (New York: Oxford University Press, 1950).

10 Genesis 3–8.

11 Reed (1999), p,8.

12 Clarke (1886).

13 Guiton (2015), p.218.

14 General Assembly of Unitarian and Free Christian Churches (2007), p.9.

15 Lester (2008), emphasis original.

16 Yearly Meeting (1999), 1.02.1.

17 Emma Nash (2014, pp. 203–4) conducted interviews with new Christians and found that for many of them Christianity was "principally about the experience of a relationship with a God who loved them".

18 Parker (2006), p.104.

19 Parker (2006), p.106.

20 Parker (2006), p.107.

21 Quoted in Ward and Wild (2002), p.145.

22 Genesis 2:25.

23 Brock and Parker (2012), p.150.

24 See McIntosh (2004), p.119.

25 My awareness of this has been raised since moving to live in Wales. Wales is a nation that some consider to be the first colony of the British Empire. It has a history shaped by colonialism. This is not to say that Wales and Welsh people, under the cover of whiteness, have not benefited from Empire at the expense of people of colour. But it does mean that there is a greater potential to recognise colonialism in all its forms by being conscious of how colonialism has shaped this nation.

26 Brock and Parker (2012), p.165.

27 Brock and Parker (2012), pp.96–8.

28 Hillesum (1996), p.319.

29 Leach (2003), p.16.

30 Muir (2016), p.6.

31 Muir (2016), p.x. Emphasis added.

32 Wilbur (1947), pp.336–7.

33 Stone (2007), p.317.

34 Quoted in Bradley (2000), pp.19–20.

35 White Maher, quoted in Muir (2016), p.136.

36 Van Ness and Concannon, quoted in Muir (2016), p.159.

37 For an exploration of the tension between church growth and the kingdom of God from a more orthodox Christian theological perspective, see Abraham (1989), pp.82–6.

6 How (not) to do evangelism

This little light of mine,
I'm gonna let it shine ...
Hide it under a bushel? No!
I'm gonna let it shine.

"This Little Light of Mine" by Harry Dixon Loes

What is evangelism?

"Why are you doing this?" was the question that I was asked at 2 a.m. one Saturday night / Sunday morning. I was standing on a bustling street in Bolton town centre. The thud-thud of dance music was rattling the windows of the bar next to me. The cold night was full of variously dressed drunk people, taxis trying to make their way between them, and neon lights. I was standing with two others in high-visibility jackets with the words "Bolton Street Angels" emblazoned on our backs. A friendly soul en route to the kebab shop had struck up a conversation with us.

"Well," I replied, "our volunteers do it for lots of different reasons. But I do it because that's my church right there." I pointed to the dark stone building at the side of the road. "And we say our purpose is to engage with the world, to love our neighbour, and this is our neighbourhood right here, so we want to make sure everyone is safe and OK in our neighbourhood."

Bolton Street Angels was an ecumenical ministry that we began at Bank Street Unitarian Chapel in Bolton a number of years ago. It grew out of a realisation that our street was really busy, but only at night, when the bars and clubs opened, and we were closed. We also realised that there were dangers for some vulnerable people, and that there were things we could do to respond to this. So we began Bolton Street Angels, offering first aid, water, flip-flops (for women who had taken high-heels off and were walking barefoot through the streets), and a friendly word to all. We most often dealt with people who had become so inebriated that they were unable to get themselves home. We offered a warm place to sober up, and a cup of tea, and often used somebody's mobile phone to contact a friend or family member who could get that person home.

Bolton Street Angels was mission. It was a deliberate act of reaching out to others, serving them, and building and seeking paradise on the streets and in the nightclubs of Bolton. It was an attempt to live out the values of love and self-less service, to let people know that they were loved, and to genuinely help people. Yet it was not evangelism, in the sense that it was not about giving a message or entering into a dialogue about religion. Nevertheless, when someone asked, "Why do you do this?", surprised as they were that we were all volunteers, they were asking a genuine question, and the genuine answer was an evangelical one: "I'm doing this because of my faith". Street Angels was always mission, but at that moment it was evangelism. Street Angels, by their actions, were always quietly witnessing to faith and love, but when I spoke aloud my reasons for doing what I was doing, I was explicitly putting into words what those actions meant in terms of faith. And the word for that is evangelism.

What is the difference between mission and evangelism? Mission is everything that the community does that seeks, discovers, or grows paradise. Mission is the community facing outwards in acts of service, peace-making, justice-making, hope-giving, and love. When Unitarians live their faith in a coherent and distinct way, it is mission. When Unitarians go on protests, it is mission. When a church raises money for a charity, it is mission. When a denomination campaigns for a change in the law of the land, it is mission. When a church hosts a project for asylum seekers, it is mission. When a church goes out on the streets and gives water to drunk people, it is mission. Mission is all of these things and many more: all those things that create or seek or reveal paradise.

Evangelism is putting the reasons for these things into words. Evangelism is attempting to explain the faith that motivates people to do mission in all these ways. Evangelism is talking about our deepest motivations for doing what we do. Evangelism is explaining the faith that is beneath it all.

Mission is the overall purpose of the church. Evangelism is just one practice of mission.[1] But how should we understand what evangelism is really all about? Researching this question, one makes an interesting discovery: there is surprisingly little published theological reflection on Christian evangelism.[2] Evangelism is a field of practical theology that struggles to be simultaneously practical and theological. Often theologians are thin on evangelism, and evangelists are thin on theology.[3] Books on the subject tend to be either huge theological tomes that are rather abstract, or church-growth manuals that ignore deeper questions of truth and meaning. What I am attempting in the rest of this book is to be both theological and practical. I want to explore the questions of theology in a comprehensive way, while also advocating concrete practices and activities.

What is evangelism? Listing synonymous words and phrases might give us some ideas:

> making religious converts
> proselytising
> recruitment
> witnessing
> sharing one's faith
> saving souls
> proclaiming the gospel
> pushing the faith
> peddling the faith
> propaganda.[4]

Many of these words and phrases have negative connotations. Many of them do not seem to fit with the Unitarian theology that we have been exploring. The nearest thing I have found to a recent definition of Unitarian evangelism is by the American John Morgan, who wrote, "Evangelism is sharing our dream with others in order to transform the world".[5]

We are in a position now to articulate what "the dream" is – the dream of paradise that we hope will transform the world. So is this definition good enough? I don't believe so. Our task up to this point has been to articulate that dream. But now we have a sense of that dream, a sense of the message, we still need to think about *how* to deliver that message. The way we deliver the message is just as important as what we say. John Morgan's definition, along with most of the others, still sees evangelism as primarily *proclamation*. It is a message given. It is something communicated in just one direction.

But a liberal evangelism must never depart from the commitment that our understanding is partial and provisional. We have a faith to proclaim, but we do not have the whole truth. We are always discovering and discerning the whole truth, so the idea of proclamation alone is inadequate. Therefore I believe that evangelism must be some form of *two-way* communication. Evangelism must be listening as well as speaking.

Liberal evangelism must be a *dialogue*. It is a dialogue when two or more people have a conversation about faith, about ultimate meaning, when people talk about what most matters to them, that in which they have trust.

Five principles for liberal evangelism

A friend of mine recently described to me an experience with Mormon missionaries at her door. She said they were friendly and polite, and she had a good talk with them for ten minutes. They invited her to a church event. She politely declined, saying she wasn't religious and she really wasn't interested. They invited her to another event. Again she declined. Eventually she had to be insistent. She took a leaflet, but firmly ended the conversation and closed the door.

As she later described this conversation to me, she said that she felt the missionaries, although polite, were pushy: they did not take no for an answer; and ultimately she felt that they might be manipulative in the way they were operating.

I am sympathetic to these objections. Many people are critical of evangelism because they have experienced evangelism being done badly. They have experienced evangelism that is coercive, aggressive, hypocritical, non-consensual, emotionally manipulative, and intellectually dishonest. But I suggest that this does not make evangelism itself an unethical practice. It simply means that evangelism is often done in a less than ethical way. This is a nuance that is rarely discussed by anyone in either common conversation or academic discourse. Writers on evangelism tend either to believe without question that it is a bad thing, or assume without question that it is a good thing. Whereas I believe we must admit that evangelism could be a very good thing, but also could be a pretty awful thing. And we must make a clear distinction between ethical evangelism and unethical evangelism, between good evangelism and bad evangelism. Fortunately the ethicist Elmer Thiessen in *The Ethics of Evangelism* has already pursued this question, and I would recommend this book for an in-depth consideration of this question. For now I would want to say that I agree with Thiessen on the need to distinguish between good evangelism and bad evangelism.

So what makes good evangelism? In some ways this is a fairly easy question to answer, as commonly agreed standards of ethics can be applied to the practice of evangelism. Good evangelism is honest and truthful, respects the integrity of individuals, is not abusive or manipulative, and contributes to human flourishing. These are commonly agreed standards of human behaviour. It is not difficult to apply them to evangelism and to call out anything that does not meet these standards as unethical evangelism.

Having set out these very basic ethical standards for evangelism, to which I would like to hold *all* people in society, I would now like to go deeper into exploring what evangelism looks like if it explicitly grows out of liberal commitments. In pursuing this question, I want to argue that means and ends should be in harmony. This is a point made by Bryan Stone in arguing that the Christian gospel is one of peace, and therefore that the practice of evangelism should be a peaceful and non-violent one. He argues, "Christian evangelism refuses every violent means of converting others to that peace, whether that violence is cultural, military, political, spiritual, or intellectual."[6] This is reminiscent of the words of Martin Luther King, Jr: "One day we must come to see that peace is not merely a distant goal that we seek, but a means by which we arrive at that goal. We must pursue peaceful ends through peaceful means."[7] If our ultimate aim is a peaceful world, then only peaceful means can be used to get there – only means that respect each individual and his or her freedom.

More specifically, we can define the faith and practice of Unitarianism by turning to a very useful essay by James Luther Adams. Adams argued for "five smooth stones of religious liberalism":[8]

1. Revelation is continuous.
2. Relations between persons ought to rest in free consent and not coercion.
3. The need to work for a just and loving world.
4. The need for ideas to be incarnated in concrete communities.
5. An ultimate attitude of hope.

I find that these principles apply very well in judging what might be an appropriate way for Unitarians to do evangelism.

First, a commitment to continuous and imperfect revelation, as we have already explored, means that evangelism is not just about *giving* paradise to the outsider on the assumption that I have it and they don't, but rather it is about *seeking* paradise together. Unitarians seek to discover truth, not merely proclaim truth; so this search will intentionally seek out the perspectives of others, because bringing in those perspectives, and engaging critically with them, will be likely to bring us closer to truth and closer to paradise.[9] This commitment to searching, not (just) giving, means that the appropriate word for this process is *dialogue*.[10]

The second principle is the liberal commitment to freedom and mutual consent in human relations, both in the church and in society.[11] This leads to a commitment to democracy, congregational polity, tolerance, and the separation of church and state. Thus free inquiry and freely chosen commitment are the best basis for discerning religious truth and forming religious community.

This means that evangelism must be done with complete honesty and openness, in a spirit of free enquiry. Evangelism must be about truth-telling. No techniques of dishonesty or coercion must be employed.[12] It is only in the context of freedom, non-coercion, and non-violence that evangelism can take place. This commitment existed at the earliest stages of Unitarian history in Transylvania. Francis David in the sixteenth century wrote: "We cannot make people accept the Gospel with weapons and threats, they obey voluntarily. There is no greater foolishness or even impossibility than wanting to externally force the conscienceness [sic] and the spirit, above which only the Creator can stand."[13]

Liberal evangelism must be done in a context of freedom and consent and honesty – a context in which the dialogue can be refused. This means, for example, "evangelising" someone in a hospital bed could be unethical, because the person cannot escape the conversation. Equally, inviting someone to a social event – a night of bingo or a quiz, for example – and then using that opportunity to push a message on that person is unethical evangelism, because it is dishonest. There was a dishonesty in inviting someone to one kind of event when it was really something quite different.[14]

Liberals may think that they don't do that kind of thing. And yet the Unitarian (and I think sometimes Quaker) tendency to "claim" historical figures often involves a twisting of the truth. When Unitarians promote themselves by saying that Isaac Newton, Charles Dickens, Florence Nightingale, or Charles Darwin were Unitarians, they are at best being very loose with the truth. I would go so far as to claim that these people were not Unitarians, and that to claim that they were is a lie. A corporate business or political party may think it is OK to manipulate the truth, or put a spin on things, for the good of their cause. But that cannot be an option for a faith community that values truth. Again I must emphasise that our means should be in harmony with our ends. Liberal evangelism must stay committed to truth.

Thirdly, liberalism affirms the moral necessity of committing to creating a more loving and just community.[15] Rooted in the conviction of the Hebrew prophets, Unitarians affirm that a ritualistic faith that does not relate to the social conditions of the society is a perverted faith. Faith should be connected to the movement of history in the direction of paradise.

Evangelism is a dialogue about faith. But faith is not only about individual spirituality or beliefs. Faith is what sustains us in the work of justice. Faith is the "radical imagination" that allows us to imagine how the world could be. In my pioneer ministry in Cardiff, I find that a great deal of my conversations with people in the city are linked to the work of justice-making. In community halls and cafés I meet with people and groups, and we talk about how to be a healthy human who works for justice locally and globally. From a liberal perspective these are evangelical conversations – conversations where there is speaking and listening about what is most sustaining and fulfilling in this work. In such conversations I witness to my faith in God and in the beauty of the world, and listen to others who witness to their deepest values as well.

Fourthly, as Adams so beautifully put it, Unitarians "deny the immaculate conception of virtue and affirm the necessity of social incarnation".[16] This means that tradition and community are inescapable in pursuing truth, and essential in pursuing justice and finding paradise. It is only groups (perhaps small groups) that have ever changed the world.

This commitment to social incarnation means that evangelism must be rooted in the life of *community*. In other words, it must closely relate to the church, it must be ecclesiological.[17] As Bryan Stone writes, evangelism "is the practice of giving the world something to see – and to touch, and to try". The world should see "a community of discipline in which the Spirit can be discerned".[18] As we have already explored, a community of paradise tries to live as an outpost of Eden in the tradition of the Celtic monasteries – a community where the Spirit is present in a people in right relationship with one another and with the world, incarnating values such as peace and hospitality and joy.

So a dialogue of faith must be a dialogue about faith community. Faith cannot be fully lived or demonstrated in isolation, though of course individual moments of evangelism may include only two people in dialogue. But at least implicitly evangelism features an invitation to community. "I'm doing this because I belong to that church," I had said to the enquirer when I was a Street Angel, literally pointing to my community building. I didn't invite him to come along in the morning (it would not have worked if I did), but I was explicit that my faith and values had been shaped by a religious community, and that indeed the service project that he was encountering was possible only because of the support of such communities.

This is one thing that was not understood by, for example, the Unitarian van missionaries of the early twentieth century. They travelled around the country in their horse-drawn van, came into a town, preached a message, then left. The message never had any strength, because it was not being incarnated in a real community, and so this was a largely ineffective Unitarian evangelistic effort. Any modern attempt at Unitarian publicity, disconnected from the witness of local communities, is likely to be equally ineffective.

Fifthly, Unitarians are optimistic about the possibility of a world of justice and peace becoming a reality within history.[19] Paradise is a reality within history today, and also a hope for the future. Paradise means faith in the goodness, meaningfulness, beauty, and holiness of life. The world is not doomed, or going to be abandoned in some divine plan for another realm. This world is good, despite all the suffering and darkness that it contains. And there is reason to hope that it can get better. Every act of service and love and activism is a witness to this hope. Hope is an expression of the radical imagination.

And so from Adams' principles of religious liberalism we can conclude that liberal evangelism should be conversational; non-coercive, and honest; rooted in the work of justice; rooted in community; and hopeful. This gives us some basic theological and practical principles for the "how" of evangelism. This gives us some sense of what it might look like to share the dream of paradise in order to transform the world. At the very least, we can say that these principles help us to know how *not* to do evangelism.

But there is one further issue to which we must return once again – and that is pluralism. Pluralism is the issue that has never been far from our considerations here, and at this point we have to address it explicitly, asking if it is possible or ethical to do evangelism in a pluralistic world.

Evangelism, pluralism, and conversion

A few months after my pioneer ministry began in Cardiff, I found myself sitting on a living-room floor with six other people chanting "Nam-myoho-renge-kyo" over and over again. We all faced a paper scroll inscribed with Chinese and Sanskrit characters in black ink, as the powerful vibration of the chant echoed around the room.

I was participating in a religious act not of my own tradition. Many conservative Christians would be very reluctant to do such a thing, but I am a liberal, always curious about other religions, and so when a friend asked if

I wanted to come along and take part in chanting in the tradition of Nichiren Buddhism, I readily agreed. We had already chatted a great deal about Jesus, the Buddha, religion in general, and how spirituality relates to activism. We were fellow pilgrims on the path of life and happy to share some religious insights and practices.

My ministry in inner-city Cardiff inevitably involves engaging with pluralism. I live in a city with Muslims, Christians, Hindus, Buddhists, Sikhs, Jews, atheists, and others. In such a city, in such a society, can I – or should I – be evangelical?

One possible liberal response is that I shouldn't be. Many liberals would recognise that all religions have value – and may even claim that "all religions are equally valid, equally true, equally salvific". If this was indeed the case, evangelism and conversion from one religion to another would be unnecessary, and perhaps even unethical.

But theologically the claim that "all religions are equally valid" is problematic. It is problematic for exactly the same reason that the claim that "only my religion is valid" is problematic. Both positions claim a certainty of religious knowledge. Both positions claim a "God's-eye view" of the universe. If we are to maintain a liberal agnosticism, we have to admit that we do not know that "only my religion is valid"; but equally we do not know for sure that "all religions are equally valid". We just do not have the ability to claim that kind of certain knowledge.

The theological argument that I have been developing here suggests that we enter dialogue seeking truth, seeking saving faith, seeking paradise, and are open to where such seeking will take us. We must be open to discovering truth and saving faith in "the other", but that is not the same thing as saying that we *know* that we will do. It is also a possibility that many people and communities might incarnate values contrary to paradise, might have beliefs that are false, or faith in something unreliable. We must acknowledge the truth of this if we think of "faith" as pointing not just to something "religious" but also to whatever a person has found to be of ultimate concern, by whatever value system they ultimately live their lives. As I have already argued, Empire is ultimately a kind of faith that asks for allegiance and worship.

We may enter into this dialogue thinking that we have found saving faith, something worthy of commitment. We may have discerned that in our experience this faith is most authentic, most reliable. It provides theological answers to our existential questions. We cannot prove that this faith is more authentic than all other possible faiths; but we are willing to enter into the dialogue.

When we enter into the dialogue, we do not know the outcome of that process. The encounter may lead to a variety of different outcomes. Let me give an example that I hope is not too simplistic. Imagine an alcoholic: one could say that her faith is alcohol: that is the ultimate orientation in her life. She reaches a crisis of faith at some point, and decides to attend meetings of Alcoholics Anonymous. There is a moment of evangelical dialogue. The dialogue leads to a conversion. As part of the programme she gives up her faith in alcohol, searches for a more authentic faith and finds Evangelical Christianity. This she finds to be a more trustworthy faith, almost literally a saving faith. She finds this faith to be so worthy of her concern that she cannot help but speak about it to others; she enters into dialogue with others who are alcoholic, confident that her faith is more authentic than theirs. She also enters into dialogue with a Zen Buddhist, confident that her faith is more authentic than his. This is also a moment of evangelical dialogue. But this dialogue is more complex: the Zen faith seems more authentic, it seems to bring about some kind of healing to the man, it is certainly a more authentic faith than the alcoholic faith.

Does this dialogue lead to a conversion? Perhaps it will. Perhaps she will discover that Zen Buddhism is a more reliable faith than Evangelical Christianity. Perhaps the Zen Buddhist will discover that Evangelical Christianity is a more reliable faith than Zen Buddhism. Perhaps both will recognise deep authenticity in each other's tradition, and will accept that much more dialogue is needed before it can be discovered which is the most authentic. Perhaps both are equally authentic. Perhaps the Evangelical Christian and the Zen Buddhist will set up a project together, supporting destitute asylum seekers, putting their different faiths together to work jointly in the same mission of serving those in need.

Throughout the whole of this scenario there has been evangelical dialogue: dialogue about faith, about ultimate concern. Three ultimate concerns (three faiths) have been in dialogue: alcoholism, Evangelical Christianity, and Zen Buddhism. All kinds of conversion, all kinds of outcome might have emerged from these evangelical dialogues.[20] But any and all of the outcomes depended on evangelical dialogue taking place. Without evangelical dialogue, the woman would not have overcome her alcoholism, without evangelical dialogue she would not have had an in-depth conversation with the Zen Buddhist, without evangelical dialogue the idea of an asylum-seekers project may never have arisen.

Yet we do not know the outcome of the evangelical dialogue beforehand. It is discovered in the process. And we must be open to this. We simply enter into dialogue open to the possibility of discovering paradise.

I believe this shows the inadequacy of defining evangelism as "trying to convert someone" to your faith. Such conversion is ultimately beyond our control. I may be "converted" by deciding for myself to trust a faith commitment. Some might say that the Truth, or God, or the Holy Spirit converts me. But what is certain is that *you* cannot convert me. You can only enter into dialogue with me. I can decide to be open to wherever that dialogue might take me. But my conversion is not within the control of another person; and if it is, if "conversion" is in some ways imposed upon me, then it is not really an authentic conversion.

It may be noted that in making this argument I am intentionally putting two things together that are usually kept apart in the theological conversation: religious pluralism/ interfaith issues and mission/ evangelism. That is because I believe that these two fields of theology are ultimately the same thing.[21]

Thus I am prepared to say that evangelism *is dialogue*. Some Christian writers try to carefully balance "witness about life in Christ" with (interfaith) "dialogue",[22] but I want to affirm that dialogue is evangelism, and evangelism is dialogue.[23] Witness about Christ (or any faith that one has found trustworthy) must involve genuine dialogue, and genuine dialogue must involve every party witnessing to their faiths. This involves both parties being open to mutual transformation[24] and both parties genuinely listening to one another.[25] I realise that this approach may be controversial, and no doubt it is not always diplomatic to talk about evangelism in interfaith contexts, but in a context where there is genuine trust and friendship, these kinds of conversation should not be avoided.

The theology that I have been attempting to construct is built on two foundations (Chapter 2 and Chapter 3): firstly that we don't have the full Truth of faith but discern it imperfectly in everyday life; and secondly that the "saving faith" that we seek is this-worldly and includes this-worldly realities of healing, awakening, flourishing, reconciliation, liberation, and justice. The language that I have used to speak about these realities is the language of paradise – where the love of God is known in reconciliation between humans and the earth.

At this point I am prepared to make the claim that *we do* discern these healing realities in some other religious traditions. That does not mean that we find such healing realities in all religions. We may not. But, for example, in my conversations and relationships with Nichiren Buddhists I have found people who clearly find peace and meaning in their faith, and take that faith into the world in ways that create justice and peace. I do not need to impose my language of faith on them, and they do not need to impose theirs on me. Both of us are enriched by living into the particularity of our own faith traditions. We can share the wisdom and practices of our faiths in a way that is mutually enriching, but we do not need to mush them together in some sort of attempt at "interfaith religion".

Is one religious faith "more true" than the other? My liberal theology forces me to answer that I simply do not know, and perhaps no one can ever know. But what I can know, in an ordinary, everyday sort of way, is that my faith feels deeply saving and authentic to me, and at the same time this other faith also seems to be deeply saving and authentic too. I can get a great deal out of dialogue and practice with Nichiren Buddhists while also being very comfortable with my own faith as a Unitarian Christian. And I can work with Buddhists, and atheists, and all kinds of people in the work of peace and justice in Cardiff and beyond.

Perhaps one day I will discern more truth in this other path. Perhaps one day I will become a Nichiren Buddhist (or a Sunni Muslim, or an atheist). As a liberal I have to admit that that is always possible. But I know that for now my commitment is to my faith in God and the world as paradise, and that feels most saving and healing and inspiring to me.

It also seems possible that different faith traditions may be working towards the same aims with different languages. In people of different faiths I do discern the same working together towards the transformation of the world. It seems to me that lots of people are working towards paradise through both the inner work of the soul and the outer work of justice. It feels to me as though anyone working on the marriage of spirituality and activism has the same mission as mine. And so there may be times when I might say to someone, "I think you should become a Buddhist", or "I think you should re-engage with your Muslim heritage". Evangelism could mean pointing someone towards a different religion if it seems that that religious faith may be most healing and enlightening to that person. It is possible to do evangelism in a non-competitive and generous way like this. We do not have to adopt a capitalistic model of competing for customers. We can adopt a model of mutual flourishing and co-operation in an abundant world. Anyone whose spirituality models a resistance to Empire is my ally.

From this attitude we can, for example, view the Unitarian mission in India as a success because it nurtured and encouraged the Brahmo Samaj, a Hindu movement, but one that was, perhaps, a more authentic faith (at least in the eyes of the Unitarians). We may not share the nineteenth-century Unitarian view that what was wrong with Hinduism was its "idolatry",[26] but we may still think that the perspectives of other faiths may lead to a deeper engagement with our own faith, or vice versa. For example, Christianity clearly had a huge effect on Mohandas Gandhi, but it did not involve him leaving his own Hindu faith.[27] It is possible to see a missionary venture, like the Unitarian one in India, as "successful" even if it did not involve any direct moves from one religion to another.[28]

So *how* should we do evangelism? The liberal answer is: non-coercively, honestly, hopefully, and within a commitment to justice and community. But above all we should do evangelism *conversationally* – in a dialogue with others where we listen as much as we speak and we are open to discovering truth and healing in words and actions of others.

What does this actually look like? In the final chapter we need to get even more specific and practical. What does this evangelical dialogue look like, and how does it function in the work of liberal communities?

Questions for reflection and discussion

1. Have you had negative experiences of evangelism?
   Positive experiences?

2. What do you think of the five principles of liberal evangelism
   – that evangelism should be conversational; non-coercive and
   honest; rooted in the work of justice; rooted in community; and
   hopeful? Would you add anything to these?

3. Is it ethical to do evangelism in a pluralistic society?

4. Are there acts of love and service that you and/or your Unitarian
   community engage in and which are identifiably rooted in
   your faith?

5. Have you ever been in a position to say "I do this because of
   my faith"? Have you ever avoided making a public connection
   between your action and your faith (because of embarrassment
   about evangelism, or for other reasons)? Could you imagine
   making the connection next time?

Endnotes

1 Bosch (1991), pp.411–2. See also Booker and Ireland (2003), pp.1–2.

2 See Abraham (1989), pp.1–2.

3 Stone (2007), p.17.

4 Thiessen (2011), pp.9, 12.

5 Morgan (1994), p.16.

6 Stone (2007), p.12.

7 King, "A Christmas Sermon on Peace" (1991b, p.255).

8 Adams (1976), pp. 12–20. However, in a conversation with George Kimmich Beach I discovered that the organising of these principles into "five smooth stones" was done by the editor Max Stackhouse, radically editing the writing of Adams.

9 Wiles (1992), p.66.

10 Dialogue is an important motif in Peers' guidelines for what Unitarian Universalist evangelism should look like, which he states comes from working with UUs in workshops. The guidelines include "Look for opportunities for dialogue ... Welcome questions ...

listen to the other person; ask probing and thoughtful questions ... Because experience is a source of our personal religion-making, listen to the other person's experience and also share your own." (Peers, 1994, pp.65–6.)

11 Adams (1976), p.14.

12 Bosch (1991), p. 413 says that evangelism "is always an invitation". Peers' guidelines for UU evangelism demonstrate this commitment when he writes "Be patient and respectful of differing views ... Be clear about our core values and demonstrate them in our approach to the conversations about faith." (Peers, 1994, p.66.)

13 Quoted in Elek (2011), p.38.

14 Other examples of deception in evangelism are found in Thiessen (2011), pp.94–5.

15 Adams (1976), p.15.

16 Adams (1976), p.17. This is affirmed by the moral philosopher Alasdair MacIntyre, who writes that "morality is always to some degree tied to the socially local and particular and that the aspirations of the morality of modernity to a universality freed from all particularity is an illusion; and ... that there is no way to possess the virtues except as part of a tradition in which we inherent them and our understanding of them" (MacIntyre, 1985, pp.126–7).

17 See Bosch (1991), p.414: "the very *being* of the church has evangelistic significance".

18 Stone (2007), pp.315–6.

19 Adams (1976), p.18.

20 Matthew Haumann writes, "I suggest that mission can also be seen as a dialogue where we share together, where we are sent to each other and share who we are. We can leave it open who gets converted by whom: maybe in sharing both parties are converted." (Quoted in Ward and Wild (2003), pp.172–3.)

21 I find it strange that dialogue with other traditions and mission seem to occupy different fields of theological reflection, when in my mind they are seeking to answer the same question. But instead of integration there seem to be only grudging nods to one another across the divide (see Bosch, 1991, pp. 474–89, Kirk, 1999, pp.118–42, and Knitter, 1996, pp.102–24, although perhaps this is a counter-example). Perhaps this is because they have come to different answers to the same question.

22 Bosch (1991), p.487.

23 Knitter (1996), p.142.

24 Knitter (1996), p.140.

25 Knitter (1996), p.145.

26 For an exploration of this issue, see W.C. Smith (1988), pp.53–68.

27 Knitter (1996), p.122.

28 Knitter (1996), p.121.

7 Dialogue as a practice of paradise

Building bridges between our divisions,
I reach out to you, will you reach out to me?
With all of our voices and all of our visions,
friends, we could make such sweet harmony.

English Quaker round
(Hymn 222 in *Sing Your Faith*)

What is dialogue?

The Unitarian theologian and philosopher Henry Nelson Wieman described his childhood growing up in Missouri as being heavily influenced by conversations with his mother. He wrote:

> When I was a boy we had long intimate talks in which each tried to express to the other what either most deeply felt and thought. We did not talk about religion particularly, but about anything which at the time seemed to be of chief concern. I would come away from those talks with a feeling of exultation, release and aspiration, as though there was something great to live for.[1]

This is an example of what I have called "evangelical dialogue": dialogue about faith, about ultimate concern. This dialogue, as Wieman demonstrates here, can be a transformational experience. It is not simply that such dialogue may lead someone to commit to faith or to a faith community. It is that the experience, the moment, of dialogue *itself* opens us to God. Dialogue is a practice of paradise, a practice that can awaken us to the reality of paradise around us.

This is beautifully demonstrated in one of the central chapters of the novel *The Color Purple* by Alice Walker. The chapter describes a conversation about the nature of God that takes place between Celie, the book's main character, and Shug Avery, the charismatic singer whom she meets. The title of the book comes from this chapter, as Shug Avery tells Celie, "I think it pisses God off if you walk by the color purple in a field somewhere and don't notice it."[2] Shug describes a God who is full of love, full of delight in creation, and present everywhere. This shocks Celie, who still has a vision of God as a white man, even though she is beginning to resent this image.

Celie begins the novel as a diminished human being, suffering from the abuse that she has endured. But it is through the encounter with Shug, and their conversations, that a transformation takes place in her. Celie opens up to a bigger experience of God and a growing sense of her own spirit and power. An encounter with another human being, a number of dialogues with another human being, open up her spirit and bring her to full humanity. That is what good evangelism looks like. This is what transformational dialogue looks like: a real encounter between humans where people come alive and encounter the divine.

In this final chapter I want to give some further real-life examples of what such transformational dialogues look like. I want to demonstrate what it looks like when we share our dream of paradise with others in order to transform the world, and how such transformation can happen. both in the invitation to community, and in the act of dialogue itself.

What is dialogue? Peter Hawkins, a contemporary British Unitarian writes:

> In dialogue ("knowing emerging between"), each person
> endeavours, while remaining true to his or her own experience,
> to be open and receptive enough to respect the reality of the other,
> within his or her own field of experience. This creates a circuit or
> flow of knowing between the participants.[3]

This requires a surrender of our assumptions and a receptiveness to the emerging meaning revealed in relationship.[4] According to the physicist and philosopher David Bohm:

> A person [entering dialogue] is ready to listen to others with
> sufficient sympathy and interest to understand the meaning of
> the other's position properly, and is ready to change his or her
> own point of view if there is good reason to do so. Evidently a
> spirit of goodwill or friendship is necessary for this to take place.
> It is not compatible with a spirit that is competitive, contentious,
> or aggressive.[5]

This dialogue must involve listening as well as speaking.[6] Each of the parties listens to the other, but also to the process itself, in which a mysterious "third power" emerges which comes from neither of the participants. Peter Hawkins writes of a "trialogue" in which the third position is the place where grace enters:

> This position, not occupied by any single individual, can be seen
> as the place of collective witness; or the opening for grace to enter;
> or, if one is a Christian, the place where the Christ-energy enters
> (*"Where two or three are gathered together in my name, there I will
> be also"* – Matthew 18:20) ... Therefore to listen to God, we have
> to listen not only to our own inner voice, not only empathetically
> to others, but also to the spaces between us; to listen for what is
> trying to emerge in the flow of conversation between us, which is
> originated by no one, and yet can illumine all parties.[7]

Such a dialogue is what I am trying to express as the liberal way of evangelism.[8] What does this look like as a practice? What could it look like? How could it be used to seek paradise and grow communities of paradise?

To answer these questions I propose to explore three different, though overlapping, kinds of dialogue. These are *nurturing dialogue, inviting dialogue*, and *pioneering dialogue*. Each of these types of dialogue exists along a spectrum in relation to the degree to which it is either internally focused on the life of the church or externally focused on the outsider. I am calling the most inwardly focused type *nurturing dialogue*, which is dialogue within the community, or perhaps with its newest members. *Inviting dialogue* is dialogue that explores, explains, or promotes the faith to outsiders. Finally, *pioneering dialogue* is a dialogue of equals without an agenda, where all may share in an open-ended fashion.

Nurturing dialogue

It was a dark winter evening a few months after I had moved to Boston, Massachusetts and joined a local Unitarian Universalist church. About ten of us gathered in the smart town house next to the church that functioned as an extension building containing offices and meeting rooms. We gathered for a shared meal and afterwards formed a circle and read out our "credo" statements. Each person described their spiritual journey, their developing theology, their understanding of God, human nature, and ethics as the conclusion to the course that had explored these topics. There was a depth and quality to the sharing that was powerful. In that room, one bitterly cold Boston evening, I was opened to paradise.

It was the last session of *Building Your Own Theology* (*BYOT*), a popular course in Unitarianism which encourages the practice of nurturing dialogue. This demonstrates that the kind of dialogue that we have been exploring can and does take place within Unitarian communities. Such dialogue involves deep sharing and listening, and opens participants to paradise within a religious community.

In the broadest sense, dialogue is the very lifeblood of every community. It takes place in worship, pastoral care, and business meetings. However, the type of dialogue that involves more existential sharing and listening will usually take place in the form of religious education classes or various forms of small-group ministry. Although such groups are not often explicitly aimed at outsiders, they are usually open to those outside the community and will sometimes be attended by new attenders or enquirers. They may function to build solidarity and trust in a community, and bring a sense of belonging to all who participate. In my experience in a large church it was the members of my *BYOT* group that became the friends to whom I would talk on a Sunday morning.

Such intentional processes of dialogue are a part of congregational life in many British Unitarian congregations. In recent years the most well used of such courses has been *Building Your Own Theology,* which was published by the American Unitarian Universalist minister, Richard Gilbert, in 1978.[9] Gilbert believed that encouraging people to form their own theology was vital for retaining them within Unitarian congregations,[10] but not expressly to attract new people. From my own experience I believe that the people most likely to take such courses are those who are new to a congregation.

BYOT is perhaps still the best-known course used in British Unitarianism, but many other similar courses have been produced, in both Great Britain and the United States.[11] In parallel with this proliferation of courses there has been what could be called a post-modern turn in the manner in which such courses are run.[12] There is now less interest in intellectual discussion and more in the development of dialogue in the sense that we have been developing above: real dialogue of faith. Unitarian minister Sarah Tinker writes that the aim of religious education should be dialogue that encourages the development of "spiritual intelligence" among participants.[13] Spiritual intelligence is characterised, among other things, by the capacity to be flexible, by self-awareness, by the capacity to face suffering, and by a reluctance to cause harm.[14] Sarah Tinker offers a vision of something that I want to identify as evangelism,

> Imagine that a few thousand Unitarians and Free Christians in the early years of the third millennium were able and willing to speak powerfully about their faith and about the value of free enquiry into religious matters. Religious education courses would help people to find their spiritual voices, encourage people to ask searching questions of themselves and one another, and enable people to clarify their values and beliefs, thus building spiritual intelligence as a contribution to the future of our species.[15]

This description demonstrates a self-transcending purpose and mission for Unitarianism. However, it does seem to be rooted in an individualistic approach that sees the only purpose of the community as supporting the individual in his or her own personal development. The theology that I have been attempting to construct here requires more than this. Faith in paradise as a self-transcending mission requires building Beloved

Communities with a distinct set of habits and spiritual practices. For this to become a reality within community would require nurturing dialogues that initiated people into these habits. A community seeking paradise would require not only general nurturing dialogue through religious education, but also dialogues of *initiation* specifically for those seeking to join the community.

Initiation is a form of dialogue that introduces a participant to a faith tradition in the context of a decision of commitment. In a mainstream Christian context, initiation may be seen in classes held in preparation for baptism or confirmation. It is striking that courses of initiation seem largely absent from Unitarian congregational life. There may be "new-member classes" in some churches, but these are somewhat rare.

This is a symptom of a Unitarianism that is rather weak on commitment and community. Joining a community is not seen as involving a huge level of demand or commitment. This is not consistent with an understanding of the saving, transforming faith in paradise, which presupposes a community of meaning and practice. If evangelism depends upon the witness of individual Unitarians living a distinctive way of life, following a saving faith, and committing themselves to a number of practices and virtues, then clearly initiation is necessary in order to induct someone into such a life.

Inviting dialogue

We can now consider a form of dialogue that is often the only kind considered to be real evangelism – what I am calling *inviting dialogue*. This is dialogue that explores, explains, or promotes the faith to outsiders, or invites them into faith or faith community. There is an element of "proclamation", but it is still in the context of dialogue.

The practice of "inviting dialogue" that is most practised and written about today is running what is called a "process evangelism course" – a course designed for newcomers to become familiar with (and committed to) the faith. Such courses have had a huge influence on thinking and practice in Christian evangelism in the last thirty years. The *Alpha* course is the most well-known process-evangelism course, and it has had a significant impact on Christianity in Britain since the 1990s.[16] The *Alpha* course is an example of Christian inviting dialogue. It consists of about fifteen talks given over a period of time, culminating in a weekend or day away.[17] It was originally developed as a course of initiation in the 1970s at Holy Trinity Brompton, an Evangelical charismatic Anglican church in London. It later developed into something more intentionally aimed at outsiders. In 1993 it was published nationally and rolled out as a course that was taken up by churches all over the country, and, eventually, the world.[18]

One report in *The Guardian* estimated that 250,000 people had come to Christian faith in the UK from *Alpha*,[19] but this number could be disputed. Other research shows that those churches running *Alpha* are less likely to decline, and more likely to grow, especially when the course has been run for three or more years.[20] Clearly such statistics are always a simplification of complex situations, and church growth is no doubt influenced by other factors too.[21] Despite presenting a theology that has been heavily criticised,[22] the success of *Alpha* demonstrates the power of small-group work and inviting dialogue as a practice.

The growth in *Alpha* and similar courses reveals an important shift that has taken place in evangelistic practice in recent years. Previously evangelism was often based on the idea of a one-off evangelistic event, in which the gospel was preached (proclamation) and people were asked to make a commitment of faith – such as the classic football-stadium Billy Graham "crusades". This approach failed to understand two increasingly important factors: first, that "conversion" is a process,[23] not an event, and secondly that people belong before they believe.[24] This means that many people will enter into a community through relationships, and only once they belong will they work out their beliefs. Process-evangelism courses are one way in which people can grow those relationships, while working out beliefs in their own time, and so they are seen as a more appropriate form of evangelism for our post-modern society.

From a liberal point of view, *Alpha* is seriously problematic in both content and style. But the principles of *Alpha* – eating together, building relationships, exploring faith in small groups – are effective and consistent with any religious liberalism. This thought has occurred to many Christians, and various parallel and alternative courses to *Alpha* have been developed in recent years, such as the *Essence* course as something more spiritual and prayerful;[25] *Living the Questions* as an "Introduction to Progressive Christianity";[26] and many more.

I have studied many of these courses, but the one that I believe most fully reflects the theology that we have been developing here is *Quaker Quest* – an outreach programme from the Religious Society of Friends. It is a "way of outreach that encourages Friends to clarify and speak of their faith experience" and "a chance for enquirers to explore issues for themselves with time given to them to do so".[27]

A number of years ago I attended a *Quaker Quest* course at a meeting house in Cheshire. Sessions began with a buffet meal, and then three speakers spoke on topics such as worship, God, and social action. The evening ended with half an hour of silent worship in the Quaker tradition. The speakers spoke powerfully in a simple, honest, and personal way about their own experiences. I think the most distinctive thing about *Quaker Quest* is its emphasis on personal faith experience. Unlike *Alpha*, there is not a single theologian or religious leader who speaks definitively on a topic, but three ordinary Quakers, who witness to their own inner experience. This demonstrates a level of trust that ordinary Quakers will be able to give messages that may be diverse or even contradictory, but will still be able to communicate something of the Quaker faith to enquirers. It is a good example of a truly liberal course of inviting dialogue. It is a course which trusts that ordinary Quakers will be able to witness to their faith and way of life, and enter into dialogue with enquirers trying to do the same.

Quaker Quest demonstrates that process-evangelism courses are effective only if they come out of a community already living the values and habits that they are proclaiming. As Bryan Stone writes, "Christians who evangelise are more important than the methods they use".[28] This is a point rarely acknowledged by anyone hoping that a process-evangelism course might be a magical off-the-shelf solution to growing a church. The effectiveness of such courses is dependent on a healthy community where members are witnessing in their way of life a transformational saving faith. People are more important than methods or techniques of church growth.

In ten years of ministry I have occasionally returned to this topic and experimented with different ways of running a Unitarian process-evangelism course of some kind. I have run these in pubs and in church buildings. I have advertised with flyers and personal invitations to new members and enquirers. I have covered topics such as Jesus, oneness, curiosity, love, justice, and religious diversity. I have spoken myself and I have invited guest speakers. I have encouraged participants to share their own stories and listen to Unitarian stories.

These experiments have produced mixed results. They have never produced a dozen new people becoming members of my church as a result of attending a course. But I believe that they did contribute to the growth and health of my congregation, as enquirers and new members attended them. But such courses are not simple, off-the-shelf, magic solutions that create church growth. They do contribute to the health and growth of congregations, but only as part of a spiritually vital worshipping community with a sense of faith and hope and mission.

When I began researching process-evangelism courses, I was of the opinion that maybe a Unitarian process-evangelism course, nationally deployed and supported, could be an effective means of denominational growth. Today I am less enthusiastic about this idea. Such inviting dialogue has much to recommend it, but it should be seen as only one small part of the mission of seeking paradise. Prayer, faith, and hope are much more important than curricula, schemes, and websites. People are more important than courses, and producing yet another course will not make much difference. It doesn't really matter what course you run – it matters what kind of church is running it.

Inviting dialogue can create moments of opening to the divine, and invite people to more deeply experience a community of faith, but many people would never attend such a course. In our secular British society the gap between the religious and non-religious is still too great, and many people will not cross the threshold to any kind of religious event. So in addition to inviting dialogue, a more pioneering dialogue is needed.

Pioneering dialogue

It was a Wednesday lunchtime in the middle of a bustling university. I was in a café in the centre of the campus, where students, staff, and visitors bought lunch, socialised with friends, or read textbooks. I had in my hand a pile of small postcard-sized pieces of paper, on which was written a brief question: "Should the UK bomb Syria?". The question was being debated in Parliament that week. It was 2015.

I approached a group of young men and put the question on their table, saying, "I'm from the Chaplaincy. It's a question for you to think about or debate today, if you would like to." They took me up on the offer and began to talk to me. I joined them and chatted with them for a few minutes. They talked about world politics, economics, and religious extremism. They were engaged, thoughtful, and opinionated. It was a good conversation, though it probably lasted only five minutes.

As a chaplain at the University of Bolton, this is what I did every Wednesday lunchtime at the university with another colleague from the Chaplaincy. We printed out a political, philosophical, or ethical question on postcards and put them out on the tables, sometimes chatting to people as we did so. Sometimes people talked to us. Sometimes they didn't. Sometimes they talked about the topic. Sometimes it became a general or pastoral or faith conversation. Sometimes they just talked among themselves about the question without involving us. But we did not force a conversation on anyone. The invitation to dialogue was refusable.

This was part of my ministry as a chaplain, and I would label this activity "pioneering dialogue", a kind of dialogue that I was intentionally organising. It was organised and planned, and yet it was deliberately open-ended and exploratory and did not present one faith tradition as the centre of the dialogue. It is worth repeating that I believe that such dialogue can truly be evangelism. It can be a transformational dialogue where faith is shared and participants seek paradise. But it is not based on running a church course or event and trying to get people to attend. It does not have a "come to us" approach, but rather a "go to them" approach. In my years in ministry I have concluded that a "come to us" approach will only ever have limited effectiveness. It is simply too difficult to get people to "come to us", and the more pioneering "go to them" approach is needed as well. Projects of pioneering dialogue can happen in public spaces, in universities, cafés, or in pubs. The initiators of a similar project in a pub wrote as follows about the ethos of what they were doing,

> People had to feel comfortable, secure and on a level playing field. This might be a church-initiated event but our aim was to listen and respond to the questions that people had, rather than start from the perspective of us telling them what we thought they needed to know.[29]

Some Christians may consider this "pre-evangelism", but I think it is proper to consider it as a form of evangelism that often involves the organisers in listening much more than in speaking.

In all of this, what matters is that there should be clarity and honesty about what kind of dialogue is taking place. If it is an open-ended dialogue of equals, then this should be made clear. If it is an inviting dialogue, in which the topic of the dialogue is one faith position, then this should be made clear. There is nothing wrong with either of these activities. What is wrong is dishonesty in suggesting that something is open-ended when in fact there is an agenda to make the conversation about the promotion of a particular faith. Therefore in pioneering dialogue the first priority needs to be to gain the trust of the participants by proving that the dialogue genuinely is open-ended and exploratory.

Unfortunately, many people have been presented with a dialogue that pretended to be exploratory and pioneering but was in fact committed inviting dialogue, trying to persuade people of the truth of a particular faith. This is the kind of dishonest unethical evangelism that gives evangelism a bad name. Because of this, ethical or liberal forms of evangelism will be treated as guilty of such deception until proven innocent, and understandably so.

In pioneering dialogue, equal time must be given to listening to the other person sharing their faith. Perhaps we are in a period where those who have historically done the most talking should spend more time listening. The evangelist Steven Croft writes about three levels of listening:

1. I listen in order to gain the right to speak;
2. I listen in order to tailor my message to what you say;
3. I listen in order to learn from your wisdom and insight.

He suggests that evangelism should involve this third level of listening.[30] Listening is evangelism.

But such pioneering evangelical dialogue does not have to be as intentional or organised as it was for me in my role as a chaplain. There have been times in my life when it has happened entirely spontaneously. In the summer before I began my first ministry, I spent a month travelling in the United States. In New York City I stayed in a youth hostel: basic, cheap, but right in the middle of Manhattan. I shared a room of bunk beds with several other men.

I got talking to one of them. He was in fact not a traveller like me but a Manhattan resident whose apartment was being fumigated, and so he was staying in the hostel for cheap accommodation for a few days. He was, in fact, one of the most interesting people I have ever met. He had had a moment of conversion a few years earlier and had given up a highly paid job in a bank, moved to New York, and now worked full time as a life model in the many art schools of Manhattan. He was much poorer and much happier. We talked about New York, about American politics, about race, and about faith.

When he found out that I was just about to start work as a minister of religion, he talked to me about his own faith and spirituality. He was not attached to any conventional religious tradition, but he had thought a lot about his sense of spirituality and the way he tried to live his life. That was a moment of spontaneous pioneering evangelical dialogue. It was not planned. It was not organised by a church. It was just two people who met and happened to open up about what was most important to them: faith. It was an opening of paradise, and something that stays very strongly in my memory.

A great deal of dialogue, perhaps most of it, can happen in many such informal and spontaneous ways. That is the way it should be. Dialogue should naturally arise when individuals or a community live provocatively, open-mindedly, and take an interest in the journeys of those with whom they come into contact.

Such dialogue may be conducted by representative persons, sometimes by virtue of simply revealing that they work for a church – sometimes on trains or planes or buses, but sometimes more deliberately, by seeking to be available and building relationships with those outside the churches. Such dialogue is not limited to ministers, of course, and it could be considered to be one of the primary callings of those who are not ministers. It may happen in all kinds of circumstances when people are open to dialogue about their faith.

Pioneering dialogue can also happen in more deliberately vocational ways. Chaplaincy is one of the roles that can allow for this kind of dialogue. Although chaplaincy is primarily about pastoral care, it is rooted in faith commitments, and pastoral conversations can of course drift into conversations about faith and ultimate concern (and sometimes it is hard to distinguish one from another). Chaplains, working within secular institutions, are of course usually at pains to say that they are *not* doing evangelism – rather they are starting with the needs of the people with whom they come into contact. This is of course appropriate and right. Chaplains should not be coercively and inappropriately forcing their faith on others. But within the ethical and liberal understanding of evangelism that we have been developing here, I would argue that what chaplains do is often a kind of pioneering evangelical dialogue where they are intentionally open to having conversations about faith and what matters most in life, and in doing so they are witnesses to their faith.

Another growing area for this kind of evangelism is pioneer ministry. This language has been used increasingly since the 2004 Church of England report *Mission-Shaped Church* recommended that the Church needed to identify, select, and train pioneer and mission entrepreneurs. Since then the Church of England, the Methodist Church, and increasingly other Christian denominations have been developing and deploying pioneer ministers with the particular mission to plant churches and develop "fresh expressions" of church with those beyond the reach of existing churches.[31]

The Church of England website defines pioneer ministers as "people called by God who are the first to see and creatively respond to the Holy Spirit's initiatives with those outside the church; gathering others around them as they seek to establish new contextual Christian community".[32] Pioneers go to those people least likely to be in church and attempt not to attract them to existing churches but to grow new expressions of church rooted in the particular culture (or subculture) of those people. Theologian and trainer of pioneer ministers Cathy Ross writes that "pioneers ... like to loiter and listen, enjoy food and drink. They are often with people on the edge of church or society, people who may not easily fit in. This takes time, intentional listening, patience – an ability to know when to wait and when to act."[33]

In 2018 I was appointed as a pioneer minister in Cardiff, in the first, and so far only, position of its kind in British Unitarianism. In addition to serving the community of Cardiff Unitarians / Undodiaid Caerdydd, I spend most of my time deliberately entering into pioneering dialogue with non-church people in inner-city Cardiff. I see my role as a return to the Unitarian missions of both Richard Wright and the urban domestic missionaries of the nineteenth century. It has been a chance to put into practice the theology that I have been attempting to develop in this book. At the time of writing, this ministry is still in its infancy, and I am in a process of learning and reflecting on my own mission to seek paradise in Cardiff in new and pioneering ways.

The foundation of this ministry is relationship-building and dialogue. Stuck on the inside of my front door is a small piece of paper that simply says, "Love neighbours. Love God." As I leave the house, this is a reminder of what I am supposed to be doing. I have found that as I commit to loving my neighbours, my neighbourhood, my city, my world, then dialogue happens spontaneously and naturally. My job at this moment is to have as much spontaneous pioneering evangelical dialogue as I can. I have these dialogues while staying mindful that my ultimate mission is to seek paradise.

Seeking paradise sometimes looks very ordinary and involves getting your hands dirty. It has involved my giving up my Sunday mornings to litter-pick with local community groups. At the other end of the local–global scale it has involved me in supporting groups campaigning against climate change. The groups with whom I have most engaged have been artists, activists, and political radicals. These are people already involved with the work to transform the world, and so the conversations have inevitably been around faith, hope, and how transformation can happen at both the global level and inner, spiritual, levels.

I very much feel that I do not have all the answers, that there is so much that I have learned from listening to others, and more still that I need to learn. I know that as a white, middle-class English man there is much that I need to learn from historically oppressed people. I find myself increasingly convinced that what I need, as well as what others need, is faith. But I do not coercively or inappropriately force a conversation of faith. Indeed, it may take months or even years of relationship building before a conversation about faith is appropriate. This is not to say that relationship building is preparation for the real work: rather, relationship building is also part of the real work. It may not be evangelism, but it is mission. Neighbourliness, community building, working together for common aims are all part of the work.

But as we struggle together against litter, or in campaigns for cleaner air in the city, or on anti-racism marches, or on pride marches, or at all kinds of other events, there are many times when questions are raised about faith, hope, and self-care. And so when appropriate I try to share my dream with others. I share my sense that another world is possible – and is already here if we have eyes to see. I share my own insights into personal spiritual practice, into my own (imperfect) attempts at daily prayer that does open me to a sense of the presence of a loving God, and give me a sense of hope.

I have found others doing much the same thing. I have had conversations with inspirational Hindu and Buddhist activists. I have had conversations in cafés with inspiring people when we have talked about the need for both inner and outer transformation and we have dreamed about how we could transform our inner-city neighbourhoods through intentional presence and neighbourliness. In such open pioneering dialogues I have felt the presence of God, the mysterious "third power" that emerges in the dialogue and seems to move us both into new dreams together.

It was from such dialogues that I was invited to contribute to a performance to mark the eightieth anniversary of the opening of the Temple of Peace and Health in Cardiff (a unique building that is both a war memorial and a civic "temple" designed to promote peace). The performance was curated by Gentle/Radical, an artist-led social-change organisation. Gentle/Radical gave participants copies of the historic order of service of the opening ceremony in 1938 and invited different people from the community to give their thoughts on it. Contributors reflected, out of their own experience, on peace, Empire, feminism, racism, and climate change. I was invited to contribute from the perspective of faith and God. I critically engaged with the aspect of the 1938 opening ceremony which praised the British Empire in the context of Christian worship. I lifted up the alternative voice, the voice rooted in the Hebrew prophets of the Bible who insisted that God was on the side of the poor and marginalised and demanded justice more than religious observance. I proclaimed my faith in a God of justice and shared my dream of a better world that is possible and within reach. From my point of view, I preached the good news. I preached the gospel to a "secular congregation" of more than one hundred and fifty people.

The point is that this opportunity to share my faith in such a loud and clear way was possible only through months of relationship building, trust, and mutual commitment to the work of others who are also doing this work of spiritual activism. Neighbourliness led to relationship, relationship led to pioneering dialogue, pioneering dialogue led to an invitation for more inviting dialogue where I more explicitly shared my faith. And this in turn led to more dialogue, as after the performance people talked to me about what I had said.

Two weeks after the performance, Gentle/Radical held a meal in a community centre to thank all their volunteers. As we shared a vegetarian curry together, we enjoyed each other's company and talked about small things and big things, about music and art and our own lives and about our dreams for the future. I looked around at those fifty people crammed into the tiny community centre and I thought to myself, "This is what paradise looks like. This is the abundant feast that Jesus was talking about. Another world is possible and is already here among us."

I have described only a few highlights from a few months' experice of pioneer ministry. I do not know what the future will hold. But I know that community is an inescapable foundation for paradise. And so my hope is that out of conversations will grow community. There is a path that leads from pioneering dialogue to inviting dialogue to the nurturing dialogue of a living community. I hope that, like a seed planted in the ground, there will be growth from dialogue to a fresh expression of church. I hope that there will be growth from my personal commitment to prayer, to a worshipping community experiencing the real presence of God. Such a community might be a visible and recognisable pattern of paradise in today's world: a community that seeks to overcome the alienation from our neighbours, the Earth, and our own bodies; a community rooted in the local culture in inner-city Cardiff and committed to the values of compassion, non-violence, hospitality, and justice; a community that acknowledges the value of other stories but is comfortable to be rooted in the particular stories of paradise. Perhaps such a community is possible.

I believe that dialogue can grow into community, and that dialogue can grow community. Pioneer ministry is the practice that attempts to grow fresh community, starting with dialogue. Pioneering dialogue creates the space of dialogue that enables faith to be explored in an open-ended fashion. Inviting dialogue can invite people into faith and existing faith community. Nurturing dialogue can sustain and support people within their commitment to faith community. Each type of dialogue has its place, and each kind of dialogue is an effective and faithful practice that can grow faith and faith community.

This is not a "how to" book about church growth. I have been intentionally trying to stay away from such pragmatic approaches. Nevertheless I am prepared to advocate dialogue as an important practice that can indeed help a congregation to grow. Whether that dialogue is nurturing or inviting or pioneering, whether it is formally organised as a course or happens spontaneously in a pub or on a bus, it is an essential practice in growing a community. I am not arguing that it is the only essential practice, or that there is not more to learn about ways of growing congregations. There is much more to learn. I am only arguing that it is one essential practice.

But I have tried to argue that the "how" of dialogue must be closely intertwined with the "why" of paradise. Dialogue depends on having something to say, a dream to share, a vision of radical imagination to speak of, a faith in something that provides an ultimate sense of hope. I have argued that the language of the kindom of God/ Beloved Community/ paradise can provide such a faith that is consistent with classical

Unitarianism. I am still on my own personal adventure in Cardiff to see how this will play out in practice. Time will tell.

Questions for reflection and discussion

1. "Dialogue itself opens us to God." Have you ever had personal experience of this – a transformative religious encounter through true openness and sharing of meaning with another person?

2. What is the significance of the fact that there is no equivalent of baptism or preparation for confirmation in Unitarianism?

3. What do you think about the effectiveness of "come to us" or "go to them" approaches to mission?

4. What does loving God and loving neighbours look like in your life and your local context?

Endnotes

1 Southworth (1995), p.9.

2 Walker (2014), p.177.

3 Hawkins (1999), p.40.

4 Hawkins, (1999), p.39.

5 Quoted in Hawkins (2006), p.104.

6 Hawkins (2006), pp.105–6 and Saxbee (1994), pp.44–5.

7 Hawkins (2006), p.107.

8 Affirming the dialogical nature of evangelism is not new. The recorded words of both Jesus of Nazareth and Paul of Tarsus are contained within the context of a dialogue, in the case of Jesus talking with people in the crowd, and in the case of Paul written correspondence. See Saxbee (1994), p.44 and Warby. Duncan MacLaren writes that "Good evangelists... are people who engage others in good conversation about important and profound topics such as faith, values, hope, meaning, purpose, goodness, beauty, truth, life after death, life before death and God." (MacLaren, 2004, p.14.)

9 Gilbert (1994), p.v.

10 Gilbert (1994), p.v.

11 They include two more American volumes of *Building Your Own Theology: Exploration* and *Ethics*; Jo Lane's *Spirituality in Everyday Life*; Keith Gilley's *Building Our Identity*; Wells' and ten Hove's *Articulating Your UU Faith*; Vernon Marshall's *The British Unitarian Journey*; and many more.

12 Perhaps it could be argued that this is a change from masculine to feminine ways of relating, as women have taken up leadership positions in the Unitarian movement.

13 Tinker (2002), p.43.

14 Tinker (2002), p.42.

15 Tinker (2002), p.44.

16 One survey found that in 1999, just six years after the publication of *Alpha*, 61 per cent of parishes in one Church of England diocese were running it or another process-evangelism course, and 20 per cent were planning to do so in the near future. (Booker and Ireland, 2003, pp.14–15.)

17 Booker and Ireland (2003), p.13.

18 Booker and Ireland (2003), p.12.

19 Warner (2007), p.115.

20 Booker and Ireland (2003), p.16 and Warner (2007), pp.117, 128.

21 Warner (2007), p.129.

22 *Alpha's* theology has been criticised for a lack of teaching on sacraments, too much stress on substitutionary atonement, too much stress on speaking in tongues, and a lack of material on social ethics. (Booker and Ireland, 2003, pp.23–7 and Warner (2007), p.122.)

23 MacLaren (2004), p.103.

24 Booker and Ireland (2003), p.17 and MacLaren (2004), p.84.

25 *Essence* "aims to give an experiential introduction to the Christian faith in a culturally relevant way" (Frost, 2002, p.11).

26 An "open-minded alternative to studies that attempt to give participants all the answers" (Procter-Murphy and Felton, 2007).

27 Yearly Meeting of the Religious Society of Friends (Quakers) in Britain (2007), p.1.

28 Stone (2007), pp.315–16.

29 Howell-Jones and Wills (2005), p.4.

30 Croft et al. (2005), p.133.

31 Baker (2014), p.2.

32 www.churchofengland.org/pioneering

33 Ross (2014), p.31.

Conclusion: reasonless hope and joy

Make me a channel of your peace.
It is in pardoning that we are pardoned,
in giving to all that we receive,
and in dying that we're born to eternal life.

Sebastian Temple, based on a prayer by Francis of Assisi
(Hymn 338 in *Hymns of Faith and Freedom*)

Two years after debating the "absolute need for numerical growth", Unitarians gathered again for their Annual Meetings. At the annual Anniversary Service the preacher was Art Lester, who preached about Unitarian growth-related anxiety. He asked the question, "Why is it that we fear we are dying?" He answered his question by suggesting that our ultimate problem was not secularisation or bad budgeting or insufficient publicity, but *a problem of the soul.*

He then quoted the Indian spiritual teacher Meher Baba: "The spiritual life is like this. Someone throws a huge snake into a crowded room. Some scream and flee in terror. Others plot and manoeuvre to avoid being bitten. And others, a very few, are filled with a reasonless hope and joy."[1] Reasonless hope and joy. It is this reasonless hope and joy that we need now more than ever. That is what paradise is like. It is a sense that, despite the darkness of the world, despite the destructive powers of Empire, *another world is possible – and indeed is already here.* That is reasonless hope and joy in the face of hopelessness.

But in the grand scheme of things the decline of one British denomination should not be the primary cause of our hopelessness. There are much bigger things to despair about. In October 2018 scientists warned that the world had twelve years to left to prevent an unprecedented climate catastrophe.[2] There is an urgent need to change our global society, otherwise we will see massive suffering for billions of people, not to mention plants and other animals. In the face of this emergency, to be primarily concerned with the fate of a tiny religious movement seems to be depressingly parochial and short-sighted.

Nevertheless I can hear a pressing question coming back to me as we end this journey: yes, but will it work? If we take on the ideas presented in this book, will it save the Unitarian community from extinction? I will continue to insist that this is the wrong sort of question to ask, but if pushed I might answer "perhaps". Perhaps developing the sort of paradise-centred communities described in this book and entering into the kind of dialogue that I have described will lead to the growth and flourishing of healthy liberal religious communities.

Or perhaps not. Perhaps the extinction of British Unitarianism (as well as several other Christian denominations) is a twenty-first-century inevitability. Perhaps the same fate is also on the cards for American Unitarian Universalism. I am not a religious sociologist, but even if I were, I know that predicting the future is a fool's game. But it is possible that the United States is just a couple of generations behind Britain in the process of secularisation. Every culture is unique and has its own path, but perhaps the same forces that have caused the decline of British Unitarianism will kick in for American Unitarian Universalism sooner than anyone realises. In Britain at least there is no doubt that a sociological shift is happening that will turn all religions into a minority. Some religious traditions will die out, but others will continue as a dynamic minority.

Which will Unitarianism be? Will it be extinct, or will it be a dynamic minority? We do not know. We cannot know. And the thing is, we need to stop worrying about it. We need to stop fearing death. Coming back to Art Lester's question, we need to ask why we are full of the fear of death. I would suggest that at least part of this fear is due to our not having faith in anything else. If all our faith is in our own institutions, then their extinction represents a crisis of faith. But if our faith is in some self-transcending purpose, if it is in paradise, where God's kindom is known on Earth, then we can remain full of reasonless hope and joy – even if our own religious institutions fail. A Unitarian publication told us as far back as 1945 that "the purpose of the Church is never merely that of self-preservation", and so it "would be better for a Church to perish as an institution than to preserve institutional life with a dead soul".[3] And so the irony and the paradox may be that the only way to grow the denomination is to *not* (ultimately) care about growing the denomination. The only way to grow the denomination is to be non-anxious and unattached to outcomes. The only way to grow the denomination is to have faith in something other than the denomination.

I believe that this is the strongest argument for the theology that I have been constructing. I am aware that there are those committed to an individualistic-pluralistic or humanistic vision for Unitarianism who may struggle to embrace the theological language that I have used here. Perhaps some may want to come to the defence of the individualistic-pluralistic model of Unitarianism that I have criticised. But the question that I would also want to ask of anyone disagreeing with me or constructing a different theological system would be – how do you keep hopeful? How do you prevent despair in a declining denomination unless you believe there is something bigger than the institution, something bigger than us, some power of grace in the world that gives us hope?

It may be that I can only really speak to those who are still committed to a classical vision of Unitarianism in this theology. If so, I am content enough. For those who have been prepared to go on this journey with me, I would plead for you to be faithful. In the face of religious decline I would continue to plead for us to be faithful – to be full of faith and hope and joy. Our liberal commitment insists that truth and salvation do not depend solely on us. Revelation is not sealed, and the light of God may yet break forth in new ways that do not depend upon us. This means that although we may *contribute* to the work of seeking truth and salvation, it does not all depend upon us. And that's a reason to relax a little. While we are here on Earth we have a responsibility to contribute to something bigger, but that greater project of seeking paradise does not have to be completed by us. What is true of a person is true of a denomination: contribute to the great work while you are alive – but don't worry, you're not the only one doing so, it does not all rest upon your shoulders.

While we are still here we do have a calling to be faithful and to continue to seek paradise, not because of our own need for self-preservation, but because of an urgent sense of the world's needs arising from climate catastrophe, poverty, racism, Empire, personal alienation, and anxiety. The world needs hope. The world needs you and me to be hopeful. Faith and faith community remain a persistent and significant source of hope for those who want to try to do something about these things. The transformation of the world depends upon the inner transformation of the soul. That is the reason why I am still evangelical: because I want to recruit people to this great work of transformation.

But faith is not a form of magic that guarantees success. It is not that the relationship of faithfulness to success is one of cause and effect. Indeed, as radical theologian John Howard Yoder has claimed, "The relationship between the obedience of God's people and the triumph of God's cause is not a relationship of cause and effect but one of cross and resurrection".[4] And so Bryan Stone has argued, "Cruciformity rather than triumph, growth, and expansion will be among the primary marks of evangelism practiced well".[5]

Faithfulness may mean reasonless hope and joy in the face of death. Faithfulness may mean facing death in the hope of resurrection. It may be that Unitarianism in its current form is dying. But perhaps it needs to die in order for some new form of religious liberalism to be born again. Religious faith does remain a significant power for transforming the world for good, and there should be a place for the kind of religion that acknowledges that revelation is not sealed, that values other religious paths, that puts love and justice above strict adherence to religious doctrines, and that sees the world as filled with the love and grace of God. Maybe such a religious faith community is waiting to be born out of the tomb of the religious community that we call Unitarian.

We do not know. And, as I say, predicting the future is foolish. But we do not need to know the future. We do not need to be successful. We need to be faithful. We need to not lose faith in the sense that another world is possible and already here: a garden of paradise where we overcome the alienation with our bodies, our neighbours, our planet, and our God. We need to share this dream with others in open and liberal conversations. We need to seek paradise with our hands, our hearts, and our voices. We need to pray as though everything depended on God, and work as though everything depended on us.

We have good news to proclaim, for ourselves and for others. The good news was described hundreds of years by the great English mystic Julian of Norwich. The good news is the truth that "all shall be well, and all shall be well, and all manner of things shall be well".[6]

Questions for reflection and discussion

1. How do you react to the idea that "the only way to grow the denomination is to not (ultimately) care about growing the denomination"?

2. Are you full of reasonless hope and joy?

Endnotes

1   Lester (2008).

2   McGrath (2018).

3   General Assembly of Unitarian and Free Christian Churches (1945), p.201.

4   Stone (2007), p.315.

5   Stone (2007), p.315.

6   Julian of Norwich, Chapter 27 (language updated).

References

Abraham, W. (1989) *The Logic of Evangelism* (London: Hodder and Stoughton).

Adams, J. L. (1976) *On Being Human Religiously: Selected Essays in Religion and Society*, edited by Max L. Stackhouse (Boston: Beacon Press).

Adams, J. L. (1986) *The Prophethood of All Believers* (Boston: Beacon Press).

Alexander, S. W. (1994) "Introduction" in *Salted with Fire: Unitarian Universalist Strategies for Sharing Faith and Growing Congregations* by Scott W. Alexander (Boston: Skinner House Books).

Baker, J. (2014) "The pioneer gift" in *The Pioneer Gift: Explorations in Mission*, edited by Jonny Baker and Cathy Ross (Norwich: Canterbury Press).

Barbauld, A.L.A. (2000) "Mrs. Barbauld's thoughts on public worship" in *Standing Before Us: Unitarian Universalist Women and Social Reform, 1776 – 1936*, edited by Dorothy May Emerson (Boston: Skinner House Books).

Beach, G. K. (2005) *Transforming Liberalism: The Theology of James Luther Adams* (Boston: Skinner House).

Bible, New Revised Standard Version, Anglicized Edition (Oxford: Oxford University Press, 1995).

Booker, M. and Ireland, M. (2003) *Evangelism – Which Way Now? An Evaluation of Alpha, Emmaus, Cell Church and Other Contemporary Strategies for Evangelism* (London: Church House Publishing).

Bosch, D. J. (1991) *Transforming Mission: Paradigm Shifts in Theology of Mission* (New York: Orbis Books).

Bradley, I. (2000) *Colonies of Heaven: Celtic Models for Today's Church* (London: Darton, Longman and Todd).

Brock, R. T. and Parker, R. A. (2012) *Saving Paradise: Rediscovering Christianity's Forgotten Love for this Earth* (Norwich: Canterbury Press).

Brown, A. J. (2006) *A Patterned Integrity: God, Jesus/the Christ and the Holy Spirit: A Prolegomena to any Future Unitarian Christian Theology* (Unitarian Christian Association Colloquium). Available at the UCA website http://www.unitarianchristian.org.uk/4.html, accessed 01/07/08.

Cassara, E. (ed.) (1997) *Universalism in America: A Documentary History of a Liberal Faith* (Boston: Skinner House Books).

Chryssides, G. (1998) *The Elements of Unitarianism* (Shaftesbury: Element Books).

Church of England website, "Vocations to Pioneer Ministry" www.churchofengland.org/pioneering, accessed 07/01/19.

Clarke, J. F. (1886) "The Five Points of Calvinism and the Five Points of the New Theology" in *Vexed Questions in Theology* (taken from http://www.tentmaker.org/articles/fivepoints.htm, accessed 05/12/18).

Cone, J. H. (1977) *God of the Oppressed* (London: SPCK).

Cooley, T. (2006) "It's not all about UUs: growth in Unitarian-Universalist congregations" in *Why Liberal Churches Are Growing*, edited by Martyn Percy and Ian Markham (London: T & T Clark International).

Courtney, C. (2002) "Outreach: a reaching in" in *Prospects for the Unitarian Movement*, edited by Matthew F. Smith (London: Lindsey Press).

Courtney, C. (2007) *Towards Beloved Community* (Liskeard: Exposure).

Croft, S. et al. (2005) *Evangelism in a Spiritual Age* (London: Church House Publishing).

Dall, C.H.A. (1857) *The Mission to India, Instituted by the American Unitarian Association* (Boston: Office of Quarterly Journal).

Darlison, B. (2002) "Encouraging congregational growth" in *Prospects for the Unitarian Movement*, edited by Matthew F. Smith (London: Lindsey Press).

Elek, R. (2011) "Contribution of Transylvanian Unitarianism to European culture: the 500th anniversary of the birth of David Ferenc" in *Faith and Freedom* Volume 64, Part 1, Number 172, pp. 34–43.

Faith and Freedom Hymn Book Working Party (1991) *Hymns of Faith and Freedom* (Chalice Press).

French, K. (2009) "The gospel of inclusion" in *UU World* (Fall 2009) https://www.uuworld.org/articles/the-gospel-inclusion, accessed 18/12/16.

Fowler, J.W. (1995) *Stages of Faith: The Psychology of Human Development and the Quest for Meaning* (New York: Harper Collins).

Frost, R. (2002) *Essence* (Eastbourne: Kingsway Publications).

Funk, R. W. et al. (1993) *The Five Gospels: The Search for the Authentic Words of Jesus* (New York, Harper Collins).

General Assembly of Unitarian and Free Christian Churches (1945) *A Free Religious Faith* (London: Lindsey Press).

General Assembly of Unitarian and Free Christian Churches (1962) *Hymns of Worship Revised* (London: Lindsey Press).

General Assembly of Unitarian and Free Christian Churches (1985) *Hymns for Living* (London: Lindsey Press).

General Assembly of Unitarian and Free Christian Churches (2007) *Annual Report 2006* (London: General Assembly of Unitarian and Free Christian Churches).

General Assembly of Unitarian and Free Christian Churches (2009) *Sing Your Faith* (London: Lindsey Press).

General Assembly of Unitarian and Free Christian Churches (2019) *Annual Report 2018* (London: General Assembly of Unitarian and Free Christian Churches).

Gilbert, R. S. (1994) *Building Your Own Theology: Volume 3: Ethics* (Boston: Unitarian Universalist Association).

Gilbert, R. S. (2000) *Building Your Own Theology: Volume 1: Introduction* (second edition) (Boston: Unitarian Universalist Association).

Gilbert, R. S. (2005) *Building Your Own Theology: Volume 2: Exploring* (second edition) (Boston: Unitarian Universalist Association).

Gilley, K. (ed.) (2002) *Building Our Identity* (Unitarian Renewal Group).

Grigg, R. (2004) *To Re-Enchant the World: A Philosophy of Unitarian Universalism* (Xlibris).

Guiton, D. (2015) *A Man that Looks on Glass: Standing up for God in the Religious Society of Friends (Quakers)* (FeedaRead Publishing).

Hall, A. (ed.) (1950) *James Martineau: Selections* (London: Lindsey Press).

Hawkins, P. (1999) "Post-modernism and religion" in *Unitarian Perspectives on Contemporary Religious Thought*, edited by George D. Chryssides (London: Lindsey Press).

Hawkins, P. (2006) "Dialogue as a form of spiritual practice" in *Being Together: Unitarians Celebrate Congregational Life*, edited by Matthew F. Smith (London: Lindsey Press).

Hill, A.M. (1994) *The Unitarian Path* (London and Edinburgh: Lindsey Press and Unitarians in Edinburgh).

Hillesum, E. (1996) *An Interrupted Life and Letters from Westerbork* (New York: Henry Holt).

Holt, A. (1936) *A Ministry to the Poor: Being the History of the Liverpool Domestic Mission Society, 1836–1936* (Liverpool: Henry Young & Sons).

Hooton, C. (2016) "The Ku Klux Klan officially endorses Donald Trump for president", *The Independent* (2 November 2016) https://www.independent.co.uk/news/world/americas/us-elections/the-ku-klux-klan-officially-endorses-donald-trump-for-president-a7392801.html, accessed 18/12/18.

Hostler, J. (1981) *Unitarianism* (London: The Hibbert Trust).

Howe, C. A. (1997) *For Faith and Freedom: A Short History of Unitarianism in Europe* (Boston: Skinner House Books).

Howell-Jones, P. and Wills, N. (2005) *Pints of View: Encounters Down the Pub* (Cambridge: Grove Books).

Hunt, S. (2004) *The Alpha Enterprise: Evangelism in a Post-Christian Era* (Aldershot: Ashgate).

Hymns of Worship (London: Lindsey Press, 1927).

Hytch, F. (2006) "The Interchange" in *The Unitarian*, May 2006, p.47.

International Missionary Council (1939) *The World Mission of the Church* (London: Livingston Press).

Jones, T. and Dawson, D. (1986) *Unisongs – A Selection of Songs for Unitarians, with Music and Chords* (London: The Religious Education and Youth Department of the General Assembly of Unitarian and Free Christian Churches).

Julian of Norwich, *Shewings*, taken from https://d.lib.rochester.edu/teams/text/the-shewings-of-julian-of-norwich-part-1, accessed 07/01/18.

Kaufman, G. D. (1993) *In Face of Mystery: A Constructive Theology* (Cambridge: Harvard University Press).

King, M. L. (1991a) "Facing the challenge of a new age" in *A Testament of Hope: The Essential Writings and Speeches of Martin Luther King Jr.,* edited by James M. Washington (New York, Harper Collins).

King, M. L. (1991b) "A Christmas Sermon on Peace" in *A Testament of Hope: The Essential Writings and Speeches of Martin Luther King Jr.* edited by James M. Washington (New York, Harper Collins).

Kirk, J. A. (1999) *What is Mission? Theological Explorations* (London: Darton, Longman and Todd).

Knitter, P. F. (1996) *Jesus and the Other Names: Christian Mission and Global Responsibility* (Oxford: Oneworld).

Lane, J. (2004) *Spirituality in Everyday Life* (London: General Assembly of Unitarian and Free Christian Churches).

Lavan, S. (1977) *Unitarians and India: A Study in Encounter and Response* (Boston: Beacon Press).

Leach, J. C. (2003) "'Something like conversion is essential': the concept of *Metanoia* in the writings of James Luther Adams", *The Journal of Liberal Religion* Vol. 4, Number 1 (Winter 2003) (http://www.meadville.edu/uploads/files/V4n1-Leach--Something-Like-Conversion-is-Essential-The-Concept-of-Metanoia-in-the-Writings-of-James-Luther-Adams-533.pdf, accessed 21/10/16).

Lester, A. (2008) "Reasonless Hope and Joy", General Assembly 80th Anniversary Sermon (2008) http://www.ukunitarians.org.uk/sermon_ga08.htm, accessed 18/12/18.

Lingwood, S. (2017) "'A definite plot of soil': a Unitarian theology of tradition", *Faith and Freedom* vol. 70, part 2, no 185 (2017) 111–24.

MacIntyre, A. (1985) *After Virtue*, second edition (London: Duckworth).

MacLaren, D. (2004) *Mission Implausible: Restoring Credibility to the Church* (Milton Keynes: Paternoster).

Marshall, V. (2004) *The British Unitarian Journey* (London: General Assembly of Unitarian and Free Christian Churches).

Marshall, V. (2007) *The Larger View: Unitarians and World Religion* (London: Lindsey Press).

Martineau, J. (1985) "Three stages of Unitarian theology" in *The Epic of Unitarianism: Original Writings from the History of Liberal Religion,* compiled by David B. Parke (Boston: Skinner House).

McGrath, Matt (2018) "Final call to save the world from 'climate catastrophe'", https://www.bbc.co.uk/news/science-environment-45775309, accessed 07/01/19.

McIntosh, A. (2004) *Soil and Soul: People Versus Corporate Power* (London: Aurum Press).

McLachlan, J. (1998) *Rara Avis: A Memoir of Richard Wright* (John McLachlan).

McLaren, B. D. (2002) *More Ready Than You Realize: Evangelism as Dance in the Postmodern Matrix* (Grand Rapids: Zondervan).

Midgley, J. (1996) *The Growing Edge* (London: Lindsey Press).

Millard, K. (2002) "Unitarian fellowship and the development of community" in *Prospects for the Unitarian Movement*, edited by Matthew F. Smith (London: Lindsey Press).

Morgan, J. (1994) "Shout it out folks: we're evangelists, too!" in *Salted with Fire: Unitarian Universalist Strategies for Sharing Faith and Growing Congregations* by Scott W. Alexander (Boston: Skinner House Books).

Muir, F. (2016) *Turning Point: Essays on a New Unitarian Universalism* (Boston: Skinner House Books).

Nash, E. (2014) "Redefining sin" in *The Pioneer Gift: Explorations in Mission*, edited by Jonny Baker and Cathy Ross (Norwich: Canterbury Press).

Parker, R. A. (2006) *Blessing the World: What Can Save Us Now*, edited by Robert Hardies (Boston: Skinner House).

Peers, L. X. (1994) "Out of the sidelines and into the main streets: steps toward an evangelical Unitarian Universalism" in *Salted with Fire: Unitarian Universalist Strategies for Sharing Faith and Growing Congregations*, by Scott W. Alexander (Boston: Skinner House Books).

Perry, H. E. (1933) *A Century of Liberal Religion and Philanthropy in Manchester: Being A History of the Manchester Domestic Mission Society, 1833–1933* (Manchester: H Rawson & Co.).

Procter-Murphy, J. and Felten, D. (writers and producers) (2007) *Living the Questions: An Introduction to Progressive Christianity* (DVD set).

Rasor, P. (2005) *Faith Without Certainty: Liberal Theology in the 21ˢᵗ Century* (Boston: Skinner House).

Reed, C. (1999) *"Unitarian? What's That?"* (London: Lindsey Press).

Reed, C., Sampson P., and Smith, M. (2007) (leaflet) *A Faith Worth Thinking About: Introducing the Unitarians* (London, Unitarian General Assembly, revised).

Roberts, J. (1978) "The Van Mission", *Transactions of the Unitarian Historical Society* Vol. XVI No. 4 (September 1978) 188–93.

Ross, C. (2014) "Pioneering missiologies: seeing afresh" in *The Pioneer Gift: Explorations in Mission*, edited by Jonny Baker and Cathy Ross (Norwich: Canterbury Press).

Saxbee, J. (1994) *Liberal Evangelism: A Flexible Response to the Decade* (London: SPCK).

Schulman, F. (2002) *James Martineau: "This Conscience-Intoxicated Unitarian"* (Chicago: Meadville-Lombard Theological School Press).

Seaburg, C. G. (1994) "Bring them hope, not hell: a short history of Universalist and Unitarian evangelism" in *Salted with Fire: Unitarian Universalist Strategies for Sharing Faith and Growing Congregations*, edited by Scott W. Alexander (Boston: Skinner House Books).

Smith, L. (2004) "The first students: the class of 1854/55" in *Unitarian to the Core: Unitarian College Manchester 1854–2004*, edited by Leonard Smith (Manchester: Carnegie on behalf of Unitarian College).

Smith, W. C. (1988) "Idolatry in comparative perspective" in *The Myth of Christian Uniqueness*, edited by John Hick and Paul F. Knitter (London: SCM).

Southworth, B. (1995) *At Home in Creativity: The Naturalistic Theology of Henry Nelson Wieman* (Boston: Skinner House).

Stone, B. (2007) *Evangelism after Christendom: The Theology and Practice of Christian Witness* (Grand Rapids: Brazos Press).

Thiessen, E. (2011) *The Ethics of Evangelism: A Philosophical Defence of Ethical Proselytizing and Persuasion* (Milton Keynes: Paternoster).

Tillich, P. (1951) *Systematic Theology: Volume I* (London: University of Chicago Press).

Tinker, S. (2002) "The future for religious education in the Unitarian movement" in *Prospects for the Unitarian Movement*, edited by Matthew F. Smith (London: Lindsey Press).

Unitarian Universalist Association (1993) *Singing the Living Tradition* (Boston: Unitarian Universalist Association).

Van Ness R., and Concannon, H. (2016) "Unitarian Universalist community cooperatives, Boston, Massachusetts: better together" in *Turning Point: Essays on a New Unitarian Universalism*, edited by Fredric Muir (Boston: Skinner House Books).

Walker, A. (2014) *The Color Purple* (London: Weidenfeld and Nicolson).

Warby, P., *A Theology of Interactive Preaching* (Anabaptist Network website http://www.anabaptistnetwork.com/node/423 accessed 21/10/16).

Ward, H. and Wild, J. (2002) *Resources for Preaching and Worship Year B* (Louisville: Westminster John Knox Press).

Ward, H. and Wild, J. (2003) *Resources for Preaching and Worship: Year C* (Louisville: John Knox Press).

Warner, R. (2007) *Reinventing English Evangelicalism, 1966–2001: A Theological and Sociological Study* (Milton Keynes: Paternoster).

Wells, B. and ten Hove, J. B. (2003) *Articulating Your UU Faith* (Boston: Unitarian Universalist Association).

White Maher, I. (2016) "Original blessing, Brooklyn, New York: a transformative spiritual relationship with the Divine" in *Turning Point: Essays on a New Unitarian Universalism*, edited by Fredric Muir (Boston: Skinner House Books).

Wilbur, E. M. (1947) *A History of Unitarianism, Vol. I: Socinianism and its Antecedents* (Cambridge: Harvard University Press).

Wiles, M. (1992) *Christian Theology and Inter-religious Dialogue* (London: SCM).

"Winchester Profession (1803)" in *Universalism In America: A Documentary History of a Liberal Faith*, 3ʳᵈ Edition, ed. Ernest Cassara (Boston: Skinner House Books, 1997).

Woolley, S. (2018) *Unitarians: Together in Diversity: A Survey of the Beliefs, Values, and Practices of Contemporary British Unitarians* (London: Lindsey Press).

Wright, R. (1824) *A Review of the Missionary Life and Labours of Richard Wright* (Liverpool: F. P. Wright) (accessed via CD Facsimile, Lensden Publishing, 2007).

Yearly Meeting of the Religious Society of Friends (Quakers) in Britain (1999) *Quaker Faith and Practice*, second edition (London: Yearly Meeting of the Religious Society of Friends (Quakers) in Britain).

Yearly Meeting of the Religious Society of Friends (Quakers) in Britain (2007) *Quaker Quest Guidelines*, obtained directly from Britain Yearly Meeting.

Lightning Source UK Ltd.
Milton Keynes UK
UKHW011832200720
366865UK00001B/28

9 780853 190943